MILLER'S

SILVER
& SHEFFIELD PLATE
MARKS

INCLUDING A GUIDE TO MAKERS & STYLES

Miller's Silver & Sheffield Plate Marks
John Bly

First published in Great Britain in 1993
by Miller's, an imprint of Octopus Publishing Group Ltd.
This edition published in 2000 by Chancellor Press,
an imprint of Bounty Books, a division of
Octopus Publishing Group Ltd,
2–4 Heron Quays, London, E14 4JP

©1993 Octopus Publishing Group Ltd
Reprinted 1994, 1995 (with corrections), 1999, 2000
Miller's is a trademark of Octopus Publishing Group Limited

Editors Janet Gleeson, Alison Macfarlane, Katie Martin-Doyle
Production Michelle Thomas
Index Hilary Bird
Marks Artworker Ian Lamont
Executive Editor Frances Gertler

The publishers will be grateful for any information which will assist them
in keeping future editions up to date. Although all reasonable care has
been taken in the preparation of this book, neither the publishers nor
the compilers can accept any liability for any consequences arising from
the use of, or the information contained herein.

A CIP catalogue record for this book is available
from the British Library

ISBN 0 75370 318 1

Set in Monotype Bembo and Gill Sans
Produced by Toppan (HK) Ltd
Printed in China

MILLER'S

SILVER
& SHEFFIELD PLATE
MARKS

INCLUDING A GUIDE TO MAKERS & STYLES

JOHN BLY

Foreword	5	Switzerland	78
		U.S.A. and Canada	79
Introduction to Silver Hallmarks			
The Development of the Silver Standard	6	**Methods of Manufacture and Decoration**	
"Milling" and the Britannia Silver Standard	9	Cast and Applied	81
Convention Marks	11	Repoussé	82
The Hallmarking Act of 1973	11	Engraving	83
Scottish and Irish Silver	12	Surface Treatments	84
Continental European Hallmarking	13	Silver Substitutes	85
Colonial Silver	14	Armorials and Cartouches	86
Unmarked Wares	15	Borders	87
Imported Silver	15		
Duty Dodgers	16	**Silver Styles**	89
Ecclesiastical Silver	16	**Illustrated Silver Styles**	
How to Read Assay Marks	17	Cake baskets	92
		Candlesticks	93
The Main British Assay Offices		Casters	94
		Coffee Pots and Chocolate Pots	95
London	18	Cruets	96
Birmingham	21	Entrée Dishes	97
Chester	23	Epergnes and Centrepieces	98
Dublin	26	Jugs	98
Edinburgh	29	Salts	99
Exeter	32	Salvers and Waiters	100
Glasgow	34	Sauce Boats	101
Newcastle	36	Spoons	102
Norwich	39	Tankards	103
Sheffield	39	Teapots	103
York	41	Tureens	104
		Two-Handled Cups	105
The Minor British Assay Offices	44	Wine Funnels	106
Barnstaple, Bristol, Carlisle, Coventry, Hull, King's Lynn, Leeds, Leicester, Lewes, Lincoln, Plymouth, Poole, Salisbury, Sherborne, Taunton, Truro		**Makers and their Marks**	
		Important British Silversmiths	107
		Other British and Irish Makers and their Marks	113
Contintental European Marks		Principal Continental Makers	155
		Other Continental Makers	159
Belgium	47	American Makers	162
Denmark	50	Other American Makers	164
France	51		
Germany	61	Gold Hallmarking	166
Italy	65	Platinum Hallmarking	167
The Netherlands	67	Sheffield Plate	168
Norway	69	Fakes and Alterations	172
Portugal	71	Collecting Silver	180
Russia	72	Glossary	182
Spain	75	Bibliography	186
Sweden	75	List of Addresses	186
		Index and Acknowledgments	187

FOREWORD

Antique silver is tangible history. It is a tactile art form and there is no better way of learning than by touch; hence the most important part of the education of the collector is the handling of as much silver as possible.

Feel how the silversmith has beaten life into his element. Feel the edges, the surface, the top and beneath. (Before established collectors raise their hands in horror, I should add that, if the silver is valuable or rare, cotton gloves should be worn.) Look obliquely against the light and see the myriad tiny scratches that produce an unfakeable patina or "skin", which has resulted from years of gentle use and care. Put yourself in the place of the silversmith and imagine how he fashioned the piece. If you are lucky enough to have inherited some silver, get to know it well; otherwise look in salerooms or antiques shops.

When you have decided where your interest lies, then venture forth and buy, modestly at first. There are bound to be fakes and alterations in any field today, but the silver collector has the hallmarking system as a guard. Nevertheless, care should be taken before embarking on a spending spree, and auctioneers, art dealers and other collectors are all surprisingly keen to advise and impart knowledge, not only to make a sale, but to encourage another member to the circle of silver devotees. As you spend time with more dealers and cataloguers you will soon find those with whom you can establish a trusting relationship.

This book is intended not only to advise new collectors, but also to provide a useful source of reference for those already experienced in the field. Although silver was first marked in 1300, the vast majority of marked wares seen on the market today date from the turn of the 17th century. Hence, the majority of marks listed in this book span from this date up to c.1939, thus covering the most important collecting period for silver. Some marks may stop earlier, if an office closed down before 1939; and in the case of major towns, later marks have sometimes been included.

INTRODUCTION

For the purposes of this book, the term "silver" refers to items made from silver metal, which from medieval times provided the coin of the realm of England, and the raw material for objects both decorative and domestic.

In its pure form, silver is too soft for normal use and it must be mixed (alloyed) with a hardening agent (alloy); predominately copper. Once alloyed, the metal is beaten out with a hammer, a hardening process called annealing. The silversmith must take care not to hit the same spot twice until the piece has been heated to realign the structure of the atoms, which are then restored to a state to withstand more beating. In this way, as a potter raises his pot and a cook his pastry, a silversmith raises his ware.

From the earliest times, objects made from silver were produced on a large scale and, as there was no standard of silver content, the description "silver" could be misleading. Early silverwares were often referred to as "wrought plate" (plate used here in the sense simply of "wares") and consisted of silver alloyed with copper. Copper was an ideal hardening agent because it did not affect the colour of the silver. It was, however, impossible to assess the purity or percentage alloy of silver with the naked eye, and the unscrupulous silversmith could add excess copper without fear of detection.

THE DEVELOPMENT OF THE SILVER STANDARD

In times of affluence a hoard of coinage could be transformed into decorative or useful silver wares, whilst in hard times such silver wares could be melted down to produce currency. It was only when goods were melted down that the dishonesty of unscrupulous silversmiths became apparent.

A system of testing was required whereby adulterated silver could be identified without melting down the objects made from it. The "touch" process then in use for testing gold, involved the scraping of the metal on a touchstone; the streaks left behind were compared to the streaks left by a piece of true gold. However, this system was insufficient for testing silver, as even adulterated metal was the same colour throughout. A more accurate test was required.

A process was therefore developed which involved

the weighing and heating of a scraping (slither or scroll) of silver in a cup of bone ash. Any copper component was absorbed into the bone ash, leaving a nugget of pure silver which was also weighed; the difference between the two weights gave a percentage adulteration. In 1300 a mark was introduced, to be applied to silverwares tested for quality (assayed). Only silver containing at least 925 parts of silver per thousand (92.5%) to 75 parts of copper (7.5%) could be termed "sterling" and receive an official stamp, or mark, as guarantee. Marking also made it easier for customs officials to prevent the export of silver from England.

Leopard's head

The stamp, known as the "King's mark", represented a lion's head. This motif was called a "*leopart*" in the heraldic French then in usage with the educated classes, and has become the leopard's head of today. Fable has it that the standard was introduced at the command of King John by a group of German silversmiths. The Germans were historically one of the Continental races referred to by the British as Easterlings, and the standard became known as the "easterling standard", which was corrupted to esterling and, supposedly, to sterling.

On 30 March, 1327, a charter was introduced by Edward III, giving royal acknowledgment to the Worshipful Company of Goldsmiths, and bestowing the right to conduct and enforce the assay laws. As assaying was to be carried out at Goldsmiths' Hall, the headquarters of the guild, the mark of guarantee was referred to as a "hallmark".

Until 1378, assay was carried out only at Goldsmiths' Hall in London and all silver had to be taken there for testing to gain the king's mark. The person was elected on an annual basis to supervise the assay and he was called the master of touch, assay master, or touch warden.

Silversmiths were often reluctant to bring their wares over long distances to London for assay. Transport in the 14th century was slow, uncomfortable and fraught with danger. Many silversmiths preferred to ignore the law and to sell their wares unmarked rather than embark on such a journey. Also, it is probable that a dishonest minority in the provinces continued to produce and sell substandard wares. This dissension threatened to undermine the guarantee of the Goldsmiths' Company; hence, in 1363, the powers of touch were granted to mayors of all cities and boroughs, whereby a representative was elected to carry out the functions of the London office *in situ*.

Prior to *c.*1350, few if any, makers had marked their wares with an identifying device, and a means was required by which an individual maker could be traced, should his wares prove substandard at assay. Thus, also in 1363, the maker's mark was legislated. As literacy was still the province of the church and the educated few, initials could not be read by the majority of the population, so simple pictorial representations were used. These were usually based on a relevant symbol, perhaps a pun on the silversmith's name or a motif taken from his shop sign.

1721   1741   1781   1801

Following the introduction, in 1363, of powers of touch to the mayors of all cities and boroughs, it became necessary to introduce a system to make the master of touch personally responsible for maintaining the silver standard. The master was re-elected annually, so from 1478 in London, silver was marked with a different letter of the alphabet each year. When the alphabet was exhausted, either the style of the letter or the form of the shield background was altered and the alphabetical cycle began again. Other town and city assay offices subsequently followed suit and introduced similar date letter marks.

Lion
passant   York   Exeter

By the beginning of the 16th century, although the standard of wrought plate was well-established, the nation's coinage, supposedly of sterling silver, had become debased. The Goldsmiths' Company decided to establish their own guarantee of quality, and in 1544 the lion *passant* mark was introduced, showing a lion seen full-figure in profile, looking over its shoulder and waving. This fast replaced the leopard's head as the sterling mark. The leopard's head became increasingly recognized as the London mark when other cities adopted their own assay marks. In York, a mark was adopted in 1560, described at the time as "the pounce of this citie, called the halfe leopard head and halfe flowre-de-luyce" (half leopard, half *fleur-de-lys*). Other cities to adopt marks at an early stage were Exeter (their cross with a crown was first used in 1575) and Edinburgh (a castle, first used in 1556). However, as the Goldsmith's guarantee of quality, the lion *passant* was used by several provincial assay offices, including York, Newcastle, Chester, Exeter and Bristol, in conjunction with their own town mark.

"MILLING" AND
THE BRITANNIA SILVER STANDARD

Until the reign of Charles II, the silver coin of the realm was hand-made and stamped. However, by the time of the Restoration the practice of "clipping" was rife. Clipping involved paring a minute piece of silver from the edge of coins until a sizeable hoard of silver was amassed, which could be forged into home-made coinage, or (since this offence was punishable by death) the stolen silver clippings were sometimes sold to a silversmith.

Britannia   Lion's head

To prevent clipping, the government had, by 1697, issued coinage with a milled edge and withdrawn the old clipped coins from circulation. In order to render silver clippings useless to a silversmith, the silver standard was raised from 925 parts per thousand (92.5%) to a purer 958.4 (95.84%), the highest possible silver content before the metal became unworkably soft. This new standard was denoted by two new marks, which replaced the leopard's head and lion *passant*; these were the lion's head erased (in heraldic terms meaning "torn from the shoulders"), still in profile, and the figure of Britannia. The new standard was therefore called the Britannia silver standard.

The increased purity of silver meant that the metal was softer and as a result different shapes began to appear (*see Silver Styles, pp89-91*). The new metal could no longer support the thinly-gauged, embossed and *repoussé* decorations popular during the Restoration, and these were replaced by more heavily-gauged forms. Items were more often cast and chased as well as engraved, and raised wares were of simple shape; thus domestic silver tended to be either extremely plain or highly decorated.

This new style of silver manufacture was already popular in France, where Huguenot silversmiths were used to working with higher quality silver. Following the Revocation of the Edict of Nantes in 1685, hoards of French protestants fled religious persecution in France, and large numbers of Huguenot craftsmen settled in Great Britain, where they practised their craft and spread their skills amongst the British.

The Britannia standard remained legal and obligatory until June 1720, when the sterling standard was reinstated by popular demand and the old sterling marks were once more used. The Britannia standard had proved comparatively expensive for both maker and buyer and had bankrupted many smaller silversmiths now consigned to the oblivion of undocumented history. Nevertheless it remained, and remains today, a legal option, although it is not in common use.

Amyé Videau

Paul Storr c.1792-1834

By the middle of the 17th century, the continued development of trade, commerce and a middle class led to vast growth in learning, and literacy was no longer the preserve of a few. From 1720 the maker's mark incorporated letters rather than a symbol. To begin with the first two letters of the maker's surname were used, but after a few years their initials were adopted.

By 1720, a hallmarking system was in operation which offered a reliable guarantee to the buying public. An indication of its effectiveness is that, today, we can tell who made a piece, what it is made of, where it was assayed and by whom, and the year of assay. It was then, and remains today, the most comprehensive recognition system in the world.

George III 1784-85

George III 1785-1820

Victoria 1837-90

Although the basic system has remained unchanged for over 270 years, other marks have come and gone. On 1 December, 1784, a tax was imposed on silver, which at one time was recorded as reaching the punitive rate of 6d an ounce. The tax was collected by the Commissioners of Stamps, the forerunners of today's Inland Revenue. Intended as a temporary duty, it was to last for 106 years, finally being abolished in 1890. To signify payment of this tax, a mark was introduced showing the sovereign's head in profile. For the first year this mark was intaglio (indented) in complete reverse of all other marks, which were struck in cameo. From 1 January, 1785, it too changed to become a cameo mark. As the assay master's mark changed in May each year, those pieces stamped in the first half of 1785 can be traced to that six-month period exactly, an unusual level of precision. Such pieces are popular with certain collectors, although this mark does not in itself add much to the value of a piece of silver.

From 1784 until 1890, five marks appeared on English silver (sterling, town, date, maker, sover-

Jubilee	Coronation	Silver Jubilee
1934-5	1952-3	1977

eign's head). From 1891 until today only four marks are used on most English silver of the sterling or Britannia standard (sterling, town, date, maker). There are three exceptions: the Jubilee mark used on pieces assayed in 1934/5 in honour of the Silver Jubilee of George V and Queen Mary; the Coronation mark, used on pieces assayed in 1953, the year of Queen Elizabeth's coronation; and the Silver Jubilee mark, an optional mark appearing on some items of over 15 grams in weight produced in 1977, the year of the Silver Jubilee of Queen Elizabeth II's accession.

CONVENTION MARKS

Common control mark

From 1 June, 1976, some special marks used at certain assay offices in the United Kingdom, Austria, Denmark, Finland, Ireland, Norway, Portugal, Sweden and Switzerland, became legally acceptable under an international convention. These include a fineness mark (Arabic numerals showing the standard in parts per thousand), a sponsor's mark, a common control mark and an assay office mark. Marks for the common European silver standard of 800 and 830 parts per thousand are also included in the convention, but these are not approved legal standards for articles sold in Britain.

THE HALLMARKING ACT OF 1973

The Hallmarking Act of 1973 rationalized many of the anomalies that existed in hallmarking law, although the silver standards remain unchanged. Each piece of silver must now be stamped with a sponsor's mark (this has largely replaced the maker's mark and shows the person responsible for manufacturing the piece), a standard mark, an assay office mark and a date letter. The standard marks are now identical at all four assay offices, except in the case of sterling silver, where the Edinburgh assay office uses a lion rampant in place of the lion *passant* used by the English offices.

SCOTTISH AND IRISH SILVER

To a large extent, Scottish and Irish silver share a history, in that both have their very early roots in the ecclesiastical silver of the Celtic church.

However, by the 12th century the Norman influence had pervaded Scotland and the prevailing taste was for artefacts in the Romanesque style. In 1457, James II of Scotland set a standard for silver of no less than eleven parts out of twelve (the equivalent of 916 parts per thousand). He also legislated a maker's mark and the mark of the dene or deacon, the chief office bearer of his craft in a town and the equivalent to the English assay master. Being an active gold or silversmith, the deacon's personal mark would be used for the duration of his tenure of office; hence a piece of this date could appear to bear two maker's marks. By 1483, a guild system had been established, with Scottish gold and silversmiths in company with other hammermen (craftsmen whose work entailed the use of a hammer) as there were not enough silversmiths to form their own substantial company. Also by 1483 the town mark was in use.

Scotland's turbulent relationship with England meant that the country's gold and, to a lesser extent, its silver, was often plundered or confiscated and not many early wares survive. It is also likely that a substantial amount was destroyed during the Reformation, and the catholic Mary Queen of Scots melted the rest down in 1567, as a result of her strife with John Knox, her Presbyterian adversary.

In 1617, the Scottish Parliament decreed that all parishes should be equipped with the basic utensils necessary for a communion service; this date marks the beginning of comprehensive documentation of silverwares in Scotland. However, Scottish secular plate is exceptionally rare until the second half of the 17th century. In 1681, a

Edinburgh from 1485

cycle of date letters was introduced that remains in use today, and in the same year the deacon's mark was replaced by the assay master's mark.

1759-1975   from1975
Edinburgh

Following the Act of Union with Scotland of 1603, the re-introduction of Sterling silver into England in 1720 meant that Scottish silversmiths had also to raise their silver standard, but this made no difference to their marking system. In 1759, the thistle mark replaced the assay master's mark, which was in turn replaced by the lion rampant in 1975. Otherwise, from the second half of the 18th century, the duty marks and optional marks used in Scotland follow those used in England.

Dublin   Hibernia

In Ireland, from 1637, silver was marked with an assay mark depicting a crowned harp. This stamp was also used as a Dublin town mark from 1637-1807. After 1807 a stamp showing the seated figure of Hibernia was used as Dublin's town mark.

CONTINENTAL EUROPEAN HALLMARKING

The English hallmarking system did not extend to the Continent of Europe, where, because of almost constant wars between nations, silver was frequently melted down to pay for armies and war debts. Europe used various standards — the only examples seen today are 800, 830 and 900 parts per thousand. These are usually shown by a small stamp somewhere on a piece. Such stamps do not necessarily correspond to contemporary English silver standards, and consequently objects with Continental marks are often sold under the name "Continental silver", or "silver-coloured metal".

In France, a form of guaranteeing mark was first used as early as 1272; however, despite the introduction of the silver standard by Charles V in 1378, the system developed haphazardly and marking remained somewhat arbitrary. French silverwares may exhibit a community mark (struck by the *gardes de la communauté* or community wardens, the equivalent of the English master of the touch, and confirming the standard of fineness), a maker's mark (usually consisting of his initials and emblem), a city mark (again, the responsibility of the community wardens) and a juranda mark (the French equivalent of the date letter system). A few other marks also appear. The charge mark, which appeared in 1672, was struck by the *fermier du droit*, or tax farmer, to confirm that any tax payable on the article had been noted and would be collected; the discharge mark confirms the payment of any such tax.

Minor marks used on French silver include the inventory or census mark. If a newly-appointed tax farmer adopted a different mark from that of his predecessor, the wares stamped by the retiring tax farmer were catalogued in a general inventory and countermarked with an inventory mark.

Silver imported to France was stamped ET, for *étranger* (foreign), while the recognition mark, introduced in 1750, was stamped on any new parts added to old pieces of silverware.

In Germany and Austria, a system was developed to denote the town of production, the maker and year letters, but these follow no reliable order. Similarly, although a silver standard existed in theory, it was not always strictly observed.

In Medieval Russia, every large monastic foundation had its own silversmith, and from the 17th century onwards all silver belonging to the patriarchs was stamped with the blessing hand. From 1613, all silver sold at fairs had to be marked, and in 1700 Peter the Great introduced a gold and silver standard to be overseen by assay offices established in all Russian towns.

Swedish silver was stamped with a mark representing the town of assay and a date letter. The Swiss system was more developed and the degrees of refinement of silver were indicated by a stamp.

Some European countries have developed a silver hallmarking system only very recently. Romania passed a law as recently as 1906 that silver must bear the maker's mark and a hallmark.

COLONIAL SILVER

Unlike Continental marks, which developed independently of the British hallmarking system, silversmiths in the British colonies, such as in Canada and the eastern seaboard of the United States, based the general form of their marks on those used in Great Britain. However, throughout much of the USA, there existed no equivalent date or town marking system, and identifying the style of a piece and its maker's mark are often the most reliable method of assessing date and authenticity (*see pp79-80 for US and Canadian marks*).

UNMARKED WARES

Over the centuries, a number of parliamentary acts in Great Britain have made it illegal to sell unmarked wares as silver, gold or platinum. However, there is in existence a substantial number of wares made before 1900 that are incompletely marked or not marked at all. There are several possible reasons for this. The piece may be part of a larger set produced strictly to commission and marked only on one piece. Alternatively, it could be part of a multi-piece item; for example a candleholder that would originally have been attached to an inkwell. Or it could simply be too small to mark. Until 1973, it was considered that any unmarked piece offered for sale should be assayed and marked. As a result some unmarked, genuine pieces were sent to assay and given modern marks which effectively destroyed an aspect of their historical importance. However, modern science has perfected the spectrographic test, whereby the precise age of a piece can be ascertained, and the assay law has been relaxed for the sake of historical interest.

In the assessment of unusual pieces without marks and with no documented provenance or information, the Antique Plate Committee plays an important role. This Committee, consisting of eight expert members of London's Goldsmiths' Hall, was established in 1939 to examine and adjudicate any piece of silver, in order to determine its authenticity and to establish whether it is in contravention of the Hallmarking Act of 1973; they are bound to qualify their reasons should they declare a piece faked or altered (*see Fakes and Alterations pp172-9*).

IMPORTED SILVER

The Customs Act of 1842 stipulated that all silver imported to Great Britain or Ireland was to be assayed and marked in a British assay office, a requirement to be backdated 42 years, to 1800. This had the disastrous effect of subjecting Continental silver to being irrelevantly stamped with Queen Victoria's head. From 1904, all imported silver had to be marked with the relevant standard in decimal — for example .925 for sterling silver, .958 for Britannia silver. The Hallmarking Act of 1973 dispensed with the decimal point and, whereas British silver of the Britannia standard is stamped 958.4 (parts per thousand), imported silver is still marked simply 958.

DUTY DODGERS

With the imposition in Britain of the punitive tax on wrought plate, from 1784-1890, there inevitably developed a number of methods of avoiding the duty. These methods of "duty dodging", as it is referred to today, are seen as separate from the innocent alterations to silverwares which have occurred over the centuries, and from faking, carried out more recently to deliberately mislead the buying public (*see Fakes and Alterations pp172-9*). Duty dodging had the sole purpose of avoiding paying the levy.

One such method involved the use of transposed hallmarks. A high quality silver piece was sent to assay; the stamped area was then removed and inserted into a piece of inferior quality. Hallmarks were also transposed from small pieces to much larger items, as the silver duty was partly based on weight.

The evidence of duty dodging is difficult to spot. One clue may be in the position of the marks, which tended to vary with fashion. For example, a Queen Anne coffee pot would usually be marked underneath the base, whereas an 18th-century coffee pot would tend to be stamped on the rim. A Queen Anne pot marked on the rim should therefore arouse suspicion.

The marks on early silver spoons (from *c*.1680-90) were randomly applied — it was not until *c*.1700 that marks began to be arranged in groups. One famous silver faker made a cast of an original early spoon, including random marks, and made a set of six spoons from the mould. The identically positioned marks gave the forger away, and he was duly punished.

ECCLESIASTICAL SILVER

Some of the finest early silver in Britain is to be found in churches. The manufacture and decoration of church plate has traditionally been of the highest standard of craftsmanship and has generally been well cared for. A certain standard of elaboration in decoration was maintained even during periods when the secular fashion was for simple, undecorated wares.

It is usually possible, with the compliance of the

local church council, to gain access to some exquisite and historical silverwares — an interesting way to see some of the oldest and finest silver crafting around, and to study some genuine and ancient marks.

Church plate is of two types — that made specially for a church, which tends to represent faithfully the high style of the day, and that given to a church as a donation from a member of the congregation or a wealthy patron. The latter type is usually of domestic style bearing an inscription, naming the donor, the church and the date of the gift. Both types add significantly to our knowledge and understanding of the silver of any given period.

The requirements for a church service have evolved over centuries and typically consist of a chalice, ewers for the wine and water, a paten and the pyx. The number of other sacred vessels and decorative objects such as candlesticks, croziers and bells depends on the size and wealth of the particular church.

The Reformation, which began as a political shift away from the Roman Catholic church, had by the 16th century developed into a vengeful force. During the devastation which followed in its wake, ecclesiastical silverwares were sorted through, and all but the items essential for Communion confiscated. To avoid this desecration, many churches melted their silver down for coinage that could be hidden and used for other purposes. Ecclesiastical pre-Reformation silver is therefore rare. As rules governing worship were relaxed over the following centuries, the amount of church silver increased.

HOW TO READ THE ASSAY MARKS ON pp18-43

Above each town's date entry is the corresponding "Hall" or "Town" mark together with the "Standard" or quality mark which would have preceded the date mark at that time. At the beginning of each entry a number of marks may be listed from before the date when the town established a formal system of marking. These are generally known only from examples found on random pieces of silver. Where no mark was found for a particular year, that year has been omitted from the list. Sometimes several marks were found for the same year and a selection of these have been shown. When a "Town" mark and "Standard" mark appear at the end of a section, this means that these two marks were used thereafter, together with the relevant date marks.

THE MAIN ASSAY OFFICES

LONDON

As early as 1180, an association of goldsmiths existed in London, although it was not legally recognized until Edward III's Act of 1327 (*see Introduction pp6-17*). This Act acknowledged the Worshipful Company of Goldsmiths, and gave them the right to enforce the assay laws. Until 1378, all silver had to be taken to Goldsmiths' Hall in the City of London for testing. Silver of the required quality was marked with the leopard's head. As other assay offices were granted powers of touch, this mark became associated with the London Assay Office. The leopard's head was surmounted by a crown between 1478 and 1821. Sometimes, between 1790 and 1820, especially on small articles, the mark was omitted altogether (*see p15*). The London goldsmiths are renowned for the very high standard of their work.

1598	1617	1636	1654
1599	1618	1637	1655
1600	1619	1638	1656
1601	1620	1639	1657
1602	1621	1640	1658
1603	1622	1641	1659
1604	1623	1642	1660
1605	1624	1643	1661
1606	1625	1644	1662
1607	1626	1645	1663
1608	1627	1646	1664
1609	1628	1647	1665
1610	1629	1648	1666
1611	1630	1649	1667
1612	1631	1650	1668
1613	1632	1651	1669
1614	1633	1652	1670
1615	1634	1653	1671
1616	1635		

Year		Year		Year		Year	
1672	P	1699	(symbol)	1727	M	1755	U
1673	Q	1700	(symbol)	1728	N	(crowned leopard)	(lion)
1674	R	1701	ff	(crowned leopard)	(lion)	1756	A
1675	S	1702	φ	1729	O	1757	B
1676	T	1703	g	1730	P	1758	C
1677	U	1704	g	1731	Q	1759	D
(leopard)	(lion)	1705	g	1732	R	1760	E
1678	a	1706	P	1733	S	1761	F
(crowned leopard)	(lion)	1707	g	1734	T	1762	G
1679	b	1708	n	1735	V	1763	H
1680	c	1709	φ	1736	a	1764	J
1681	d	1710	p	1737	b	1765	K
1682	e	1711	q	1738	C	1766	L
1683	f	1712	r	(crowned leopard)	(lion)	1767	M
1684	g	1713	s	1739	d d	1768	N
1685	h	1714	t	1740	e	1769	O
1686	i	1715	u	1741	f	1770	P
1687	k	1716	A	1742	g	1771	Q
1688	l	1717	B	1743	h	1772	R
1689	m	1718	C	1744	i	1773	S
1690	n	1719	D	1745	k	1774	T
1691	o	(crowned leopard)	(lion)	1746	l	1775	U
1692	p	1720	E	1747	m	1776	a
1693	q	1721	F	1748	n	1777	b
1694	r	1722	G	1749	o	1778	c
1695	s	1723	H	1750	p	1779	d
1696	t	1724	I	1751	q	1780	e
(crowned leopard)	(lion)	(crowned leopard)	(lion)	1752	r	1781	f
1697	a b	1725	K	1753	s	1782	g
1698	c	1726	L	1754	t	1783	h

Year	Letter	Year	Letter	Year	Letter	Year	Letter
	(shields)	1812	R	1839	D	1869	O
1784	i	1813	S	1840	E	1870	P
1785	k	1814	T	1841	F	1871	q
	(shields)	1815	U	1842	G	1872	r
1786	l	1816	a	1843	H	1873	s
1787	m	1817	b	1844	J	1874	t
1788	n	1818	C	1845	K	1875	u
1789	O	1819	d	1846	L	1876	A
1790	P	1820	e	1847	M	1877	B
1791	q	1821	f	1848	N	1878	C
1792	r		(shields)	1849	O	1879	D
1793	S	1822	g	1850	P	1880	E
1794	t	1823	h	1851	Q	1881	F
1795	u	1824	i	1852	R	1882	G
1796	A	1825	k	1853	S	1883	H
1797	B	1826	l	1854	T	1884	I
1798	C	1827	m	1855	U	1885	K
1799	D	1828	n	1856	a	1886	L
1800	E	1829	o	1857	b	1887	M
1801	F	1830	p	1858	c	1888	N
1802	G	1831	q	1859	d	1889	O
1803	H	1832	r	1860	e	1890	P
1804	I	1833	s	1861	f		(shields)
1805	K		(shields)	1862	g	1891	Q
1806	L	1834	t	1863	h	1892	R
1807	M	1835	u	1864	i	1893	S
1808	N	1836	A	1865	k	1894	T
1809	O	1837	B	1866	l	1895	U
1810	P		(shields)	1867	m		(shields)
1811	Q	1838	C	1868	n	1896	a

Year	Mark	Year	Mark	Year	Mark	Year	Mark
1897	b	1917	a	1936	A	1957	b
1898	c	1918	b	1937	B	1958	c
1899	d	1919	d	1938	C	1959	d
1900	e	1920	e	1939	D	1960	e
1901	f	1921	f	1940	E	1961	f
1902	g	1922	g	1941	F	1962	g
1903	h		🦁	1942	G	1963	h
1904	i	1923	h	1943	H	1964	i
1905	k	1924	i	1944	I	1965	k
1906	l	1925	k	1945	K	1966	l
1907	m	1926	l	1946	L	1967	m
1908	n	1927	m	1947	M	1968	n
1909	o	1928	n	1948	N	1969	o
1910	p	1929	o	1949	O	1970	p
1911	q	1930	p	1950	P	1971	q
1912	r	1931	q	1951	Q	1972	r
1913	s	1932	r	1952	R	1973	s
1914	t	1933	s	1953	S	1974	t
1915	u	1934	t	1954	T		🦁
	🦁	1935	u	1955	U		
1916	a		🦁	1956	a		

BIRMINGHAM

The Birmingham office began assaying in 1773, having been convened by an Act of Parliament in 1772. Birmingham's mark shows an upright anchor and is usually accompanied by a lion *passant*, a date letter and a duty mark (the sovereign's head), and the maker's initials. Birmingham marks are often seen on smallwares, such as vinaigrettes, snuff-boxes and buckles.

	Mark	Year	Mark	Year	Mark	Year	Mark
	🦁 ⚓	1775	C	1778	F	1781	I
1773	A	1776	D	1779	G	1782	K
1774	B	1777	E	1780	H	1783	L

	1812	O	1840	R	1869	U
1784	M	1813	P	1841	S	1870	V
1785	N	1814	q	1842	T	1871	W
	1815	r	1843	U	1872	X
1786	O	1816	s	1844	V	1873	Y
1787	P	1817	t	1845	W	1874	Z
1788	Q	1818	u	1846	X		
1789	R	1819	V	1847	Y	1875	a
1790	S	1820	W	1848	Z	1876	b
1791	T	1821	X		1877	c
1792	U	1822	y	1849	A	1878	d
1793	V	1823	z	1850	B	1879	e
1794	W	1824	A	1851	C	1880	f
1795	X	1825	B	1852	D	1881	g
1796	Y	1826	C	1853	E	1882	h
1797	Z	1827	D	1854	F	1883	i
1798	a	1828	E	1855	G	1884	k
1799	b	1829	F	1856	H	1885	l
1800	c	1830	G	1857	I	1886	m
1801	d	1831	H	1858	J	1887	n
1802	e	1832	J	1859	K	1888	o
1803	f	1833	k	1860	L	1889	p
1804	g		1861	M	1890	q
1805	h	1834	L	1862	N		
1806	i	1835	M	1863	O	1891	r
1807	J	1836	N	1864	P	1892	s
1808	k	1837	O	1865	Q	1893	t
1809	l		1866	R	1894	u
1810	m	1838	P	1867	S	1895	v
1811	n	1839	Q	1868	T	1896	w

Year	Mark	Year	Mark	Year	Mark	Year	Mark
1897	X	1917	S	1938	O	1958	J
1898	y	1918	t	1939	P	1959	K
1899	z	1919	u	1940	Q	1960	L
⚓ 🦁		1920	v	1941	R	1961	M
1900	a	1921	w	1942	S	1962	N
1901	b	1922	X	1943	T	1963	O
1902	c	1923	y	1944	U	1964	P
1903	d	1924	Z	1945	V	1965	2
1904	e	1925	A	1946	W	1966	R
1905	f	1926	B	1947	X	1967	S
1906	g	1927	C	1948	Y	1968	T
1907	h	1928	D	1949	Z	1969	U
1908	i	1929	E	⚓ 🦁		1970	V
1909	k	1930	F	1950	A	1971	W
1910	l	1931	G	1951	B	1972	X
1911	m	1932	H	1952	C	⚓ 🦁	
1912	n	1933	J	1953	D	1973	Y
1913	o	1934	K	1954	E	⚓ 🦁	
1914	p	1935	L	1955	F	1974	Z
1915	q	1936	M	1956	G	⚓ 🦁	
1916	r	1937	N	1957	H		

CHESTER

There are records in town deeds of silversmiths working in Chester as early as the 13th century. Marking of silver was not regulated until the end of the 17th century, even though there was a guild of goldsmiths who supervised the manufacture, assay and sale of plate from the early 15th century.

Chester's town mark showed a shield bearing the arms of the city. The accompanying marks were similar to those of London of the same period, with the lion *passant*, leopard's head and date letter. The majority of silverware found now bearing the Chester mark consists of smallware such as tankards, beakers, tumblers and cream jugs. The office stopped operating on 24 August 1962.

Year	Mark	Year	Mark	Year	Mark	Year	Mark
1683	STERLING	1715	P	1743	S	1772	V
1685	Sterlin	1716	Q	1744	T	1773	W
1686	(shields)	1717	R	1745	U	1774	X
1687	(shields)	1718	S	1746	V	1775	Y
1688	(shields)	1719	T	1747	W		(shields)
1689	(shields)	1720	U	1748	X	1776	a
1690-2	(shields)	1721	V	1749	Y U	1777	b
1690-2	(shield)	1722	W	1750	Z	1778	c
1690-2	STERLING	1723	X		(shields)	1779	d
1692	STERLING	1724	Y	1751	a	1780	e
1692-4	STERLING	1725	Z	1752	b	1781	f
1695-1700	STERLING		(shields)	1753	c	1782	g
1695	D	1726	A	1754	d	1783	h
1696	E	1727	B	1755	e		(shields)
1697	F	1728	C	1756	f	1784	i
	(shields)	1729	D	1757	G	1785	k
1701	A	1730	E	1758	h	1786	l
1702	B	1731	F	1759	i	1787	m
1703	C	1732	G	1760	k	1788	n
1704	D	1733	H	1761	l	1789	o
1705	E	1734	I	1762	m	1790	p
1706	F	1735	K	1763	n	1791	q
1707	G	1736	L	1764	O	1792	r
1708	H	1737	M	1765	P	1793	s
1709	I	1738	N	1766	Q	1794	t
1710	K	1739	O	1767	R	1795	u
1711	L	1740	P	1768	S	1796	v
1712	M	1741	Q	1769	T		(shields)
1713	N	1742	R	1770	U	1797	A
1714	O			1771	U		

Year	Mark	Year	Mark	Year	Mark	Year	Mark
1798	B	1825	G	1854	O	1883	U
1799	C	1826	H	1855	R		(marks)
	(marks)	1827	I	1856	S	1884	A
1800	D	1828	K	1857	T	1885	B
1801	E	1829	L	1858	M	1886	C
1802	F	1830	M	1859	N	1887	D
1803	G	1831	N	1860	W	1888	E
1804	H	1832	O	1861	T	1889	F
1805	I	1833	P	1862	Q		(marks)
1806	K	1834	Q	1863	Z	1890	G
1807	L	1835	R		(marks)	1891	H
1808	M	1836	S	1864	a	1892	I
1809	N	1837	T	1865	b	1893	K
1810	O	1838	U	1866	c	1894	L
1811	P		(marks)	1867	d	1895	M
1812	Q	1839	A	1868	e	1896	N
1813	R	1840	B	1869	f	1897	O
1814	S	1841	C	1870	g	1898	P
1815	T	1842	D	1871	h	1899	Q
1816	U	1843	E	1872	i	1900	R
1817	V	1844	F	1873	k		(marks)
	(marks)	1845	G	1874	l	1901	A
1818	A	1846	H	1875	m	1902	B
1819	B	1847	I	1876	n	1903	C
1820	C	1848	K	1877	o	1904	D
1821	D	1849	L	1878	p	1905	E
1822	D	1850	M	1879	q	1906	F
	(marks)	1851	A	1880	r	1907	G
1823	E	1852	O	1881	s	1908	H
1824	F	1853	P	1882	t	1909	I

1910	🄺	1919	🄣	1927	🄑	1935	🄡
1911	🄛	1920	🄤	1928	🄒	1936	🄢
1912	🄜	1921	🄥	1929	🄟	1937	🄦
1913	🄝	1922	🄦	1930	🄔	1938	🄐
1914	🄞	1923	🄧	1931	ff	1939	🄞
1915	🄟	1924	🄨	1932	🄖		
1916	🄠	1925	🄩		🕷 ⛨ 🄖		
1917	🄡		🕷 ⛨	1933	🄗		
1918	🄢	1926	🄐	1934	🄘		

DUBLIN

Although Dublin's city council decreed that silver
of the correct standard (coin) was to be marked with a
lion, a harp and a castle, Irish silver was only sporadically
marked. In 1637 a crowned harp with a date letter was
introduced, with a maker's mark system being introduced in 1638; marked examples survive from that date
onwards. In 1731 the figure of Hibernia was introduced,
and in 1807 the monarch's head was added as the duty
mark, giving Dublin five marks until 1890, when the
monarch's head was again dropped. The Dublin mark is
found on a wide variety of silver wares, and Irish workmanship is acclaimed for its excellent decorative style.
After the Revocation of the Edict of Nantes in 1685,
many Huguenot goldsmiths emigrated to Dublin, bringing Continental influences to Irish silver which lasted
throughout much of the 18th century.

1638	👑🛡 𝕬		👑🛡		👑🛡		👑🛡
	👑🛡	1646	𝗜	1655	**S**	1663	**f**
1639	**B**	1647	**K**	1656	**T**	1664	**g**
1640	**B**	1648	**L**	1657	**U**	1665	**h**
1640	**C**	1649	**M**	1658	**a**	1666	**i**
1641	**D**	1650	**N**		👑🛡	1667	**k**
1642	**E**	1651	**O**	1659	**b**	1668	**l**
1643	**F**	1652	**P**	1660	**c**	1669	**m**
1644	**G**	1653	**Q**	1661	**d**	1670	**n**
1645	**H**	1654	**R**	1662	**e**		👑🛡

Year	Mark	Year	Mark	Year	Mark	Year	Mark
1671	O	1708	T	1735	P	1763	P
1672	p	1709	U	1736	Q	1764	Q
1673	q	1710	a	1737	R	1765	R
1674	r	1711	a	1738	S	1766	S
1675	s	1712		1739	T	1767	T
1676	t	1713		1740	UU	1768	U
1677	u	1714	E			1769	W
1678	A	1715	F	1741	W	1770	X
		1716	Z	1742	X	1771	Y
1679	B			1743	Y	1772	Z
1680	C	1717	a	1744	Z		
1681	D	1718	b	1745		1773	A
1682	E	1719	c	1746	Z	1774	B
1683	F					1775	C
1685-7	G	1720	A	1747	A		
		1721	B	1748	B	1776	D
1688	H	1722	C	1749	C	1777	E
1692	I	1723	D	1750	D	1778	F
		1724	E	1751	EE	1779	G
1693-5	K	1725	F	1752	F	1780	H
1696-9	L	1726	G	1753	G	1781	I
		1727	H	1754	H	1782	K
1700	M	1728	J	1755	H	1783	L
1701	N	1729	k	1757	U	1784	M
1702	O	1730	L	1758	K	1785	N
1703	Q			1759	U	1786	O
1704	R	1731	L				
1705	R	1732	M	1760	M	1787	P
1706	S	1733	N	1761	N	1788	Q
1707	S	1734	O	1762	O	1789	R

Year	Letter		Year	Letter		Year	Letter		Year	Letter
1790	S		1817	W		1838	S		1862	T
1791	T		1818	X		1839	T		1863	S
1792	U		1819	Y		1840	U		1864	T
1793	W		1820	Z		1841	V		1865	U
1794	X		1821	A		1842	W		1866	V
1795	Y		1822	B		1843	X		1867	W
1796	Z		1823	C		1844	Y		1868	X
1797	A		1824	D		1845	Z		1869	Y
1798	B		1825	E e		1846	a		1870	Z
1799	C		1826	F		1847	b		1871	A
1800	D		1827	G		1848	C		1872	B
1801	E		1828	H		1849	d		1873	c
1802	F		1829	I		1850	e		1874	D
1803	G		1830	K		1851	f f		1875	E
1804	H		1831	L		1852	g g		1876	F
1805	I		1832	M		1853	h h		1877	G
1806	K		1833	N		1854	j		1878	H
1807	L		1834	O		1855	k		1879	U
1808	M		1835	P		1856	l		1880	K
1809	N		1836	Q		1857	m		1881	L
1810	O		1837	R		1858	n		1882	M
1811	P					1859	O		1883	N
1812	Q					1860	P		1884	O
1813	R					1861	Q		1885	P
1814	S								1886	Q
1815	T								1887	R
1816	U								1888	S
									1889	T

1890	U	1903	(mark)	1916	(A)	1930	(P)
1891	V	1904	(mark)	1917	(b)		
1892	W	1905	(mark)	1918	(C)	Up to 1931 the date letter was changed on 1st June. The Q of 1932 began on 1st January	
1893	X	1906	(mark)	1919	(D)		
1894	Y	1907	(mark)	1920	(e)		
1895	Z	1908	(A)	1921	(F)	1932	(Q)
(mark) (mark)		1909	(O)	1922	(S)	1933	(R)
1896	A	1910	(P)	1923	(h)	1934	(S)
1897	B	1911	(Q)	1924	(I)	1935	(T)
1898	C	1912	(R)	1925	(B)	1936	(U)
1899	D	1913	(S)	1926	(C)	1937	(V)
1900	E	1914	(T)	1927	(m)	1938	(W)
1901	F	1915	(U)	1928	(n)	1939	(X)
1902	G	(mark) (mark)		1929	(O)		

EDINBURGH

Silverwares bearing Scottish hallmarks survive from the mid-16th century. The silver standard had been established in Scotland in 1457, by James II of Scotland. At the same time the deacon or warden (the chief office bearer of the craft within the city) was charged with upholding the silver standard and his mark was used as the assay mark. Edinburgh's town mark showing a castle was added in 1485. A sequence of date letters was not introduced until 1681, when the deacon's mark was also replaced by the assay master's mark. A thistle was introduced in 1759 as the standard mark to replace the assay master's mark and is found on all Edinburgh hallmarked silver plate up until 1975. Scotland was not subject to the Britannia Standard, but when sterling was restored in England in 1720, the standard of silver was raised in Scotland to the same level of purity and 6d. an ounce tax was also levied. The Edinburgh mark can be found on an extensive range of domestic and ecclesiastical plate.

1609	(mark) (R)	1617	(G)	1633	(mark) (A)	1642	(F)
1611	(mark) (D)		(mark)	1637	(N)		(mark)
	(mark)	1613-21	(mark)		(mark) (mark)	1643	(F)
1617-19	(IL)	1616	(G)	1640	(T)	1644	(A)

Year	Mark	Year	Mark	Year	Mark	Year	Mark
1649-57	GG	1699	t	1728	Y	1758	D
1651-9	IF	1700	u	1729	Z		[castle] [trident]
1660	VB	1701	w	1730	A	1759	E
1663-81	IC	1702	x	1731	B	1760	F
1665-7	IS	1703	y	1732	C	1761	G
1665	IS	1704	z	1733	D	1762	H
1669-75	R		[castle]	1734	E	1763	I
	[castle] B	1705	A	1735	F	1764	K
1681	a	1706	B	1736	G	1765	L
	[castle] B	1707	C	1737	H	1766	M
1682	b	1708	D	1738	I	1767	N
1683	c	1709	E	1739	K	1768	O
1684	d	1710	F	1740	L	1769	P
1685	e	1711	G	1741	M	1770	Q
1686	f	1712	H	1742	N	1771	R
1687	g	1713	I	1743	O	1772	S
1688	h	1714	K	1744	P	1773	T
1689	i	1715	L	1745	Q	1774	U
1690	k	1716	M	1746	R	1775	W
1691	l	1717	N	1747	S	1776	X
1692	m	1718	O	1748	T	1777	Y
1693	n	1719	P	1749	U	1778	Z
1694	o	1720	Q	1750	V	1779	V
1695	p	1721	R	1751	W	1780	A
	[castle] P	1722	S	1752	X	1781	B
1696	q	1723	T	1753	Y	1782	C
1697	r	1724	U	1754	Z	1783	D
	[castle] r	1725	V	1755	A		[castle] [trident]
1698	s	1726	W	1756	B	1784	E
		1727	X	1757	C	1785	F

Year	Mark	Year	Mark	Year	Mark	Year	Mark
(shield marks)		1815	J	1843	(A)	1873	R
1786	G	1816	k	1844	(A)	1874	S
1787	G	1817	l	1845	(O)	1875	T
1788	H	1818	m	1846	(P)	1876	U
1789	IJ	1819	n	1847	(Q)	1877	V
1790	K	(shield marks)		1848	(R)	1878	W
1791	L	1820	O	1849	(S)	1879	X
1792	M	1821	P	1850	(T)	1880	Y
1793	N	1822	q	1851	(U)	1881	Z
1794	O	1823	r	1852	(V)	1882	a
1795	P	1824	S	1853	(W)	1883	b
1796	Q	1825	t	1854	(X)	1884	c
1797	R	1826	u	1855	(Y)	1885	d
1798	S	1827	V	1856	(Z)	1886	e
1799	T	1828	W	1857	A	1887	f
1800	U	1829	X	1858	B	1888	g
1801	V	1830	y	1859	C	1889	h
1802	W	1831	Z	1860	D	1890	i
1803	X	1832	A	1861	E	(shield marks)	
1804	Y	1833	B	1862	F	1891	k
1805	Z	1834	C	1863	G	1892	l
1806	a	1835	D	1864	H	1893	m
1807	b	1836	E	1865	I	1894	n
1808	C	1837	f	1866	K	1895	o
1809	d	1838	g	1867	L	1896	p
1810	e	1839	h	1868	M	1897	q
1811	f	1840	J	1869	N	1898	r
1812	g	(shield marks)		1870	O	1899	s
1813	h	1841	k	1871	P	1900	t
1814	i	1842	l	1872	Q	1901	u

Year		Year		Year		Year	
1902	w	1921	Q	1940	K	1959	B
1903	T	1922	R	1941	L	1960	C
1904	U	1923	S	1942	M	1961	F
1905	3	1924	T	1943	N	1962	G
1906	A	1925	U	1944	O	1963	H
1907	B	1926	V	1945	P	1964	I
1908	C	1927	W	1946	Q	1965	k
1909	D	1928	X	1947	R	1966	l
1910	E	1929	Y	1948	S	1967	m
1911	F	1930	Z	1949	T	1968	n
1912	G	1931	A	1950	U	1969	o
1913	H	1932	B	1951	V	1970	P
1914	I	1933	C	1952	W	1971	Q
1915	K	1934	D	1953	X	1972	R
1916	L	1935	E	1954	Y	1973	S
1917	M	1936	F	1955	Z	1974	S
1918	N	1937	G	1956	A		
1919	O	1938	H	1957	B		
1920	P	1939	I	1958	C		

EXETER

The earliest Exeter assay mark dates back to the mid-16th century and consists of the letter X, usually in a round shield with a crown on top. In 1701 this town mark changed to a three-towered castle. Between 1701 and 1720 the town mark was accompanied by the maker's mark, the Britannia mark, and the lion's head erased. In 1721 this was replaced by the leopard's head and the lion *passant* in square shields. Assay marking in Exeter was erratic until *c.*1700, and although many craftsmen are known to have worked in the region, little surviving silver bears the Exeter mark. After 1700, the marks are found on a wide range of ecclesiastic and domestic wares. The office closed in 1883.

Year		Year		Year		Year	
1600		c. 1600	X			1620	b
1600		1606	X	1610	a	1620	X

1620	1703 C	1731 g	1760 M
c.1630	1704 D	1732 h	1761 N
c.1630	1705 E	1733 i	1762 O
c.1635	1706 F	1734 k	1763 P
c.1635	1707 G	1735 l	1764 Q
1635	1708 H	1736 m	1765 R
1640	1709 I	1737 n	1766 S
1640	1710 K	1738 o	1767 T
1640	1711 L	1739 p	1768 U
1640	1712 M	1740 q	1769 W
1640	1713 N	1741 r	1770 X
1640-50	1714 O	1742 s	1771 Y
1640-50	1715 P	1743 t	1772 Z
1640-50	1716 Q	1744 u	
1640-50	1717 R	1745 w	1773 A
1646-98	1718 S	1746 v	1774 B
1670 X	1719 T	1747 y	1775 C
1676	1720 V	1748 z	1776 D
1676			1777 E
1680 XON IV	1721 W	1749 A	Leopard's head not used after 1777
1680	1722 X	1750 B	
1690 EX ON	1723 Y	1751 C	1778 F
1690	1724 Z	1752 D	1779 G
1690		1753 E	1780 H
1690	1725 a	1754 F	1781 I
1690	1726 b	1755 G	1782 J
1698 X	1727 c	1756 H	1783 K
	1728 d	1757 I	1784 L
1701 A	1729 e	1758 K	1785 M
1702 B	1730 f	1759 L	1786 N

Year		Year		Year		Year	
1787	O	1812	Q	1836	u	1859	C
1788	P	1813	R	1837	A	1860	D
1789	Q	1814	S	1838	B	1861	E
1790	R	1815	T	1839	C	1862	F
1791	S	1816	U	1840	D	1863	G
1792	T	1817	a	1841	E	1864	H
1793	U	1818	b	1842	f	1865	I
1794	W	1819	c	1843	G	1866	K
1795	X	1820	d	1844	H	1867	L
1796	Y	1821	e	1845	I	1868	M
1797	A	1822	f	1846	K	1869	N
1798	B	1823	g	1847	L	1870	O
1799	C	1824	h	1848	M	1871	P
1800	D	1825	i	1849	N	1872	Q
1801	E	1826	k	1850	O	1873	R
1802	F	1827	l	1851	P	1874	S
1803	G	1828	m	1852	Q	1875	T
1804	H	1829	n	1853	R	1876	U
1805	I	1830	o	1854	S	1877	A
1806	K	1831	P	1855	T	1878	B
1807	L	1832	q	1856	U	1879	C
1808	M	1833	T	1857	A	1880	D
1809	N	1834	S	1858	B	1881	E
1810	O	1835	t			1882	F
1811	P						

GLASGOW

Glasgow had its own corporation of hammermen by 1536, and in 1681 they adopted a date letter system. However, this went out of use in the early 18th century, when the letters S (Sterling, or Scottish), O and E were frequently used, together with the town mark showing a tree with a bird in its upper branches, a bell suspended from a lower branch and a fish laid at the base. In 1819 the lion rampant of Scotland and the sovereign's head were added, and in 1914 the thistle standard mark was used. The Glasgow office closed in 1964, after running at a loss for some years. Silver marked with the early Glasgow hallmark is rarely seen.

Date	Mark	Date	Mark	Date	Mark	Date	Mark
1681	a	1702	w	1763-70	F	1827	I
1682	b	1703	x	1773-80	S S	1828	J
	(mark)	1704	y	1776-80	(mark) O	1829	K
1683	c	1705	z	1776-80	(mark) O	1830	L
1684	d	1706	A	1776-80	(mark)	1831	M
1685	e		(mark)	1776-80	(mark) S	1832	N (mark)
1686	f	1707-8	B	1783	(mark)	1833	O
1687	g	1709	D	1783	(mark) S	1834	P
1688	h	1710	D	1777-90	(mark) S	1835	Q
	(mark)		(mark) D	1782-92	(mark)	1836	R
1689	i	1709-20	(mark)		(mark)		(marks)
1690	k	1728-31	S	1785-95	S	1837	S
1691	l	1725-35	S	1785-95	O	1838	T
1692	m		(mark)	1781	(mark) S	1839	U
1693	n	1743-52	S	1811-3	(mark)	1840	V
	(mark)	1747-60	S	1819	A	1841	W (mark)
1694	o	1756-76	S		(marks)	1842	X
1695	p	1756-76	S	1820	B	1843	Y
1696	q	1757-80	(mark)	1821	C	1844	Z
1697	r	1757-80	(mark)				(marks)
1698	(marks) S		(mark)	1822	D	1845	A
1699	(marks) t	1757-80	(mark)	1823	E	1846	B
	(mark)	1758-65	S	1824	F	1847	C
1700	u		(mark)	1825	G	1848	D
1701	v	1763-70	F	1826	H	1849	E

1850	F	1873	C	1897	A	1921	y
1851	G	1874	D	1898	B	1922	z
1852	H	1875	E	1899	C		
		1876	F	1900	D	1923	a
1853	I	1877	G	1901	E	1924	b
1854	J	1878	H	1902	F	1925	c
1855	K	1879	I	1903	G	1926	d
1856	L	1880	J	1904	H	1927	e
1857	M	1881	K	1905	J	1928	f
1858	N	1882	L	1906	K	1929	g
1859	O	1883	M	1907	K		
1860	P	1884	N	1908	L	1930	h
1861	Q	1885	O	1909	M	1931	i
1862	R	1886	P	1910	N	1932	j
1863	S	1887	Q	1911	O		
1864	T	1888	R	1912	P	1933	k
1865	U	1889	S	1913	Q	1934	l
1866	V	1890	T			1935	m
1867	W	1891	U	1914	R		
1868	X	1892	V	1915	S	1936	n
1869	Y	1893	W	1916	T	1937	o
1870	Z	1894	X	1917	U	1938	p
		1895	Y	1918	V	1939	q
1871	A	1896	Z	1919	W		
1872	B			1920	X		

NEWCASTLE

Newcastle was granted power of assay by Henry VI's statute of 1423. The original mark was three separate castles in a shield. Marking was rather erratic until 1702 when the figure of Britannia and the lion's head erased, denoting the new standard, were introduced. In 1720, when the old standard was restored, the leopard's head and lion *passant* replaced the old mark, used with the town mark and date letter. From 1721 to 1727 the lion

passant faces to the right. Substantial quantities of
Newcastle silver date from the early 18th century,
especially domestic ware, such as coffee pots and teapots.
Large numbers of tankards and two-handled cups were
also produced in this city. The last assay of silver at
Newcastle was in April 1884.

1658	1702	1726
1664	1703	1727
1668	1704	Between 1721-8 shapes of shields and lion *passant* vary; the lion may face left
no mark found for 1669	1705	
1670-2	1706	
1672	1707	1728
1675	1708	1729
1680	1709	1730
1684	1710	1731
1684	1711	1732
1684	1712	1733
1685	1713	1734
1685	1714	1735
1686-7	1715	1736
1686-8	1716	1737
1692	1717	1738
1694	1718	1739
1694	1719	1740
1694	1720	1741
1695	1721	1742
1697	1722	1743
1698	1723	1744
1698-9	1724	1745
1700	1725	1746
1701		1747
1748	1756	1764
1749	1757	1765
1750	1758	1766
1751	1759	1767
1752	1760	1768
1753	1761	1769
1754	1762	1770
1755	1763	1771
		1772
		1773

1774 H	1801 L	1830 Q	1858 T
1775 I	1802 M	1831 R	1859 U
1776 K	1803 N	1832 S	1860 W
1777 L	1804 O	1833 T	1861 X
1778 M	1805 P	1834 U	1862 Y
[shields]	1806 Q	1835 W	1863 Z
1779 N	1807 R	1836 X	[shields]
1780 O	1808 S	1837 Y	1864 a
1781 P	1809 T	1838 Z	1865 b
1782 Q	1810 U	[shields]	1866 c
1783 R	1811 W	1839 A	1867 d
1784 S	1812 X	1840 B	1868 e
1785 T	1813 Y	1841 C	1869 f
1786 U	1814 Z	1842 D	1870 g
1787 W	[shields]	1843 E	1871 h
1788 X	1815 A	1844 F	1872 i
1789 Y	1816 B	1845 G	1873 k
1790 Z	1817 C	[shields]	1874 l
[shields]	1818 D	1846 H	1875 m
1791 A	1819 E	1847 I	1876 n
1792 B	1820 F	1848 J	1877 o
1793 C	1821 G	1849 K	1878 p
1794 D	1822 H	1850 L	1879 q
1795 E	1823 I	1851 M	1880 r
1796 F	1824 K	1852 N	1881 s
1797 G	1825 L	1853 O	1882 t
1798 H	1826 M	1854 P	1883 u
1799 I	1827 N	1855 Q	
[shields]	1828 O	1856 R	
1800 K	1829 P	1857 S	

There were at least a dozen silversmiths active in
Norwich as early as the 13th century. Norwich was
granted power of assay by Henry VI's statute of 1423.
The original mark showed a castle surmounting a lion
passant, and wares were also stamped with the date letter
and the maker's mark. In the first part of the 17th century a mark depicting a crowned, seeded rose was introduced, to be replaced in the last half of the century by
a stemmed rose. Assaying of silver in Norwich was spo-
radic and probably ceased altogether after 1701. From
remaining examples it seems that the city specialized in
church plate and spoons of a high standard.

Date	Marks	Date	Marks	Date	Marks	Date	Marks
1600	🅻	1630	🅶	1642	🜓	1680	🛡🛡🛡
1610	🛡🛡🛡	1631	H	1643	V	1685	🛡🛡
1620	🛡🛡🛡	1632	🅸	1645	✚ 🜨	1688	🛡🛡🛡
1620	🛡 👑	1633	🅺	1645	🛡🛡🛡	1688	🛡🛡
1620	🛡	1634	🅻	1653	🛡🛡🛡	1689	🅱
1624	🛡🛡🛡	1635	M	1661	🛡🛡🛡	1690	C
1624	🛡🛡	1636	N	1661	🛡🛡🛡	1691	D
1624	A	1637	🛡🛡		🛡	1692	E
1625	B	1637	O	1670	🛡🛡	1693	F
1625	🛡	1638	P	1670	🛡	1694	G
1626	C	1639	🛡🛡	1670	🛡🛡🛡	1695	H
1627	D	1639	Q	1670	🛡🛡🛡	1696	I
1627	🛡	1640	R	1675	🛡🛡🛡	1697	🛡🛡🛡
1628	🛡	1641	S	1676	🛡		
1629	F			1679	🛡		

SHEFFIELD

By the middle of the 18th century, Sheffield was a
major manufacturing centre for silver. The efforts of
Matthew Boulton, a Birmingham industrialist, led to
the Act of Parliament in which Sheffield was established as an assay office in 1773. Until 1974, Sheffield's
mark depicted a crown which featured along with the
usual marks used at other assay offices. Date letters were
first used in 1773, starting with E, and changed irregu-
larly each year until 1824. After this date they were
arranged in alphabetical order. Sheffield hallmarks can
be found on all types of domestic plate. The region was
renowned for candlesticks; many were bought by
other silversmiths who superimposed their own marks.

Year	Mark		Year	Mark	Year	Mark	Year	Mark
	🦁👑		1800	N	1830	g	1858	P
1773	Œ		1801	H	1831	h	1859	R
1774	F		1802	M	1832	k	1860	S
1775	(letter)		1803	F	1833	I	1861	T
1776	R		1804	G	🦁👑◯		1862	U
1777	h		1805	B	1834	m	1863	V
1778	S		1806	A	1835	P	1864	W
1779	A		1807	S	1836	q	1865	X
1780	C		1808	P	1837	r	1866	Y
1781	D		1809	K	1838	S	1867	Z
1782	G		1810	L	1839	t	🦁👑◯	
1783	B		1811	C	🦁👑◯		1868	A
🦁👑			1812	D	1840	u	1869	B
1784	I		1813	R	1841	V	1870	C
1785	V		1814	W	1842	X	1871	D
🦁👑◯			1815	O	1843	Z	1872	E
1786	k		1816	T	1844	A	1873	F
1787	T		1817	X	1845	B	1874	G
1788	m		1818	I	1846	C	1875	H
1789	(letter)		1819	V	1847	D	1876	J
1790	L		1820	Q	1848	E	1877	K
1791	P		1821	Y	1849	F	1878	L
1792	u		1822	Z	1850	G	1879	M
1793	o		1823	U	1851	H	1880	N
1794	m		1824	a	1852	I	1881	O
1795	q		1825	b	1853	K	1882	P
1796	Z		1826	C	1854	L	1883	Q
1797	X		1827	d	1855	M	1884	R
1798	V		1828	e	1856	N	1885	S
1799	E		1829	f	1857	O	1886	T

1887	**U**	1909	**r**	1930	**n**	1953	**L**
1888	**V**	1910	**s**	1931	**O**	1954	**M**
1889	**W**	1911	**t**	1932	**P**	1955	**N**
1890	**X**	1912	**u**	1933	**Q**	1956	**O**
	🐾 🦁	1913	**v**	1934	**r**	1957	**P**
1891	**Y**		👑 🦁	1935	**s**	1958	**Q**
1892	**Z**	1914	**w**	1936	**t**	1959	**R**
1893	**a**	1915	**x**	1937	**u**	1960	**S**
1894	**b**	1916	**y**	1938	**v**	1961	**T**
1895	**c**	1917	**z**	1939	**w**	1962	**U**
1896	**d**		👑 🦁	1940	**X**	1963	**V**
1897	**e**	1918	**a**	1941	**y**	1964	**W**
1898	**f**	1919	**b**	1942	**Z**	1965	**X**
1899	**g**	1920	**C**	1943	**A**	1966	**Y**
1900	**h**	1921	**d**	1944	**B**	1967	**Z**
1901	**i**	1922	**e**	1945	**C**	1968	**A**
1902	**k**	1923	**f**	1946	**D**	1969	**B**
1903	**l**	1924	**g**	1947	**E**	1970	**C**
1904	**m**	1925	**h**	1948	**F**	1971	**D**
1905	**n**	1926	**j**	1949	**G**	1972	**E**
1906	**o**	1927	**k**	1950	**H**	1973	**F**
1907	**p**	1928	**l**	1951	**I**	1974	**G**
1908	**q**	1929	**m**	1952	**K**		■ 🦁

YORK

The earliest evidence of silver-making in York dates
from the 14th century. As one of the major provincial
centres in England at the time, it was granted power of
assay by Henry VI's statute of 1423, but there is evidence
of the existence of a local touch from as early as 1410.
The original mark was a half leopard's head with a *fleur-
de-lys* joined together in one shield, followed with a
sequence of date letters and makers' marks. The half
leopard's head was replaced by a half-seeded rose by the
end of the 17th century and in 1701, it was changed to

five lions *passant* on a cross, but the office was virtually
dormant by this time, and closed in 1856. So far no
pieces have yet been found that bear a date mark
between 1713 and 1778. Early York silver showed fine
craftsmanship, often reflecting Scandinavian design.
Silverwares after 1700 tended to be less refined.

Year	Mark	Year	Mark	Year	Mark	Year	Mark
1607	🛡 A	1629	P	1652	U	1673	R
	🛡	1630	Z	1653	w	1674	S
1608	B	1631	🛡 a	1654	X	1675	T
1609	C		🛡	1655	y	1676	U
1610	D	1632	b	1656	Z	1677	V
1611	E	1633	c	1657	🛡 A	1678	W
1612	F	1634	d	1658	🛡 B		🛡
	🛡	1635	e		🛡	1679	X
1613	G	1636	🛡 f	1659	C	1680	Y
1614	H		🛡	1660	D	1681	Z
	🛡	1637	g	1661	E		🛡
1615	I	1638	h	1662	🛡 F	1682	A
1616	K	1639	i		🛡	1683	B
1617	L	1640	j	1663	G		🛡
1618	M	1641	k	1664	H	1684	C
1619	N	1642	l	1665	J	1685	D
1620	O	1643	m		🛡	1686	E
1621	P	1644	n	1666	K	1687	F
1622	🛡 Q	1645	o	1667	L	1688	G
1623	🛡 R	1646	p	1668	M	1689	H
1624	🛡 S	1647	q	1669	N	1690	J
	🛡	1648	r		🛡		🛡
1625	T	1649	🛡 s	1670	O	1691	K
1626	U		🛡	1671	P	1692	L
1627	W	1650	t	1672	Q	1693	M
1628	x	1651	u			1694	N

Year	Mark	Year	Mark	Year	Mark	Year	Mark
	(symbol)	1783	H	1808	W	1834	r
1695		1784	J	1809	X	1835	
1696		1785	K	1810	Y	1836	
1697		1786	L	1811	Z	(symbols)	
1698	R	(symbols)		(symbols)		1837	A
1699	S	1787	A	1812	a	1838	B
(symbols)		1788	B	1813	b	1839	C
1700		1789	C C	1814	c	1840	D
1701	B	1790	d	1815	d	1841	E
1702	C	1791	e	1816	e	1842	F
1703	D	1792	f	1817	f	1843	G
1704	D	1793	g	1818	g	1844	H
1705	F	1794	h	1819	h	1845	I
1706	G	1795	i	1820	i	1846	K
1707	G	1796	k	1821	k	1847	L
1708		1797	L	1822	l	1848	M
1709		1798	M	1823	m	1849	N
1710		1799	N	1824	n	1850	O
1711		1800	O	1825	o	Leopard's head not used after 1850	
1712		1801	P	1826	p		
1713		1802	Q	1827	q	1851	P
(symbols)		1803	R	1828	r	1852	Q
1778	C	1804	S	1829	s	1853	R
1779	D	1805	T	1830	t	1854	S
1780	E	1806	U	1831	u	1855	T
1781	F	1807	V	1832	v	1856	V
1782	G	(symbol)		1833	w		

THE MINOR ASSAY OFFICES

Barnstaple

Goldsmiths are known to have worked in Barnstaple as early as 1370 and they are regularly recorded until the end of the 17th century. The earliest mark used by goldsmiths from 1272 until 1624/5 was adapted from the borough mark, which showed a bird in a circular stamp. The mark later changed to a triple-turreted tower derived from the city's arms and was used until the end of the 17th century.

Bristol

The city was granted power of assay by Henry VI's statute of 1423 and was also appointed an Assay Office by the Act of 1701. However, there are no traces of an assay office or of a guild of goldsmiths. This seems remarkable in a city that had its own long-established mint. There have been some marks found with the Bristol arms (a ship issuing from a castle) included, but their origin is not yet confirmed.

Carlisle

Marks dating from the 16th and 17th century, showing a single four-petalled rose, have been identified as the marks of the city of Carlisle. A similar rose appears in the arms of the city.

Coventry

The city was granted power of assay by Henry VI's statute of 1423. A guild of goldsmiths flourished here in the Middle Ages, but there is little evidence now of the work of these craftsmen. There is some uncertainty as to the city's mark. It was thought to be an animal in outline, possibly an elephant, but this was later attributed to the Devon and Cornwall goldsmiths. There are four pewter plates which bear the Coventry arms, but little further evidence that this was their mark.

Hull

Hull was not included in the 1423 Act, giving cities outside of London the powers of touch, although the quality of work that survives shows that many highly-skilled craftsmen must have worked in the region. Early pieces made in Hull are marked with the letter H as town mark; this was replaced in the 17th century by the town arms showing three ducal coronets. It is unlikely that there was an assay office here, but its distance from London and other towns made the registering of its own marks practical.

King's Lynn

Following popular practice, the town arms of King's Lynn were adapted to make the town mark. This shows three dragons' heads with crosses in their mouths on a shield background. Marks have been recorded from here from *c*.1632.

Leeds

As was common practice amongst the provincial silversmiths, Leeds' goldsmiths adopted the arms of the town, showing a golden fleece, for its town mark. The mark is usually found on wares dating from the 17th century.

Leicester

Silversmiths were active in Leeds from the early 16th century until the 17th century. The town mark depicted a cinquefoil, taken from the city's coat of arms.

Lewes

Lewes' silversmiths marked their wares with a chequered shield derived from the town seal, which showed a lion rampant in the right-hand corner. Spoons bearing this mark survive from the late 16th and early 17th century.

Lincoln

The city was granted power of assay by Henry VI's statute of 1423, although silversmiths are known to have worked in Lincoln from the 12th century onwards. The town mark was derived from the city arms and depicted a *fleur-de-lys*. The mark is most commonly found on spoons.

Plymouth

Plymouth marks date from *c.*1600–*c.*1700, when the city's arms were adapted to make a town mark showing a saltire between four castles. This mark is usually found on spoons. From the early 18th century the goldsmiths of Plymouth used the assay office of Exeter to register marks.

Poole

Marks depicting a scallop shell, dating from the 16th and 17th centuries, have been identified as the coat of arms of Poole. Three similar shells appear in the town arms.

Salisbury

The city was granted power of assay by Henry VI's statute of 1423. However, there are no marks found which can be definitely associated with this city and there is no evidence of a guild of goldsmiths. Some spoons were found in various parts of Wiltshire which bear marks which have been ascribed to Salisbury.

Sherborne

Although there is no known town mark, there are records of one famous local goldsmith, Richard Orenge, who used marks from 1572 to 1607 which depicted his initials and a central pellet, surrounded by two concentric circles of pellets.

Taunton

Evidence of goldsmiths using the town mark of a 'T' and a tun can be found on apostle spoons and a paten, dating between 1665 and 1689.

Truro

A mark showing the initials TR surrounded by a circle of pellets found on Cornish spoons of the 17th century is thought to be the town mark of Truro.

EUROPEAN, AMERICAN AND CANADIAN SILVER MARKS

The selected marks illustrated below represent the most commonly-seen silver marks from the other major European centres of silvermaking and the United States and Canada. (*For Britain and Ireland see pp18-46.*)

BELGIUM

From the mid-16th century, silversmiths in Brussels, Artois (Northern France, now Belgium), Luxembourg and the Netherlands were regulated by order of Emperor Charles V. By the 17th century silver was marked with a town mark, date letter and maker's mark. Hallmarking became obligatory in 1831. After 1869 assaying was no longer customary and any standard of purity was permitted. State marks indicating purity were introduced.

Antwerp Variations on this mark used from the early 16th to late 18th century.

early 18thC

A date letter system was used between the 17th and 18th centuries.

Bruges Similar marks used between the early 16th and 18th centuries.

1660 1777 17thC 18thC

Brussels Similar marks used between the 17th and 18th centuries.

1658   1764   early 18thC

Ghent Similar marks used between the 16th and late 18th centuries.

early 18thC   1752   1787

Liège Various marks within a shield used between the 16th and 18th centuries. Sometimes date appears in mark.

1688/94   1693   1744

1764   1784

Louvain A key or a shield surmounted by a crown used between the 15th and 18th centuries. Letter *B* or *V* is also sometimes found.

1710   18thC   1777

Mons Similar mark or letters *AE* surmounted by a crown used between the 15th and 18th centuries. Last two letters of date surmounted by crown also sometimes found.

1730   1750   1766

1776/9   1779   1793

Tournai Castle turret, letter *T* surmounted by a crown, or three *fleurs-de-lys* surmounted by a crown used between the 16th and 18th centuries. Last two letters of date surmounted by crown also used.

early 18thC

1737 **1740** **1781**

Ypres Similar marks used between the early 16th century and mid–18th centuries. Letter *Y* surmounted by crown used in the late 18th century.

1701/13 **1712**

1745-50 **late 18thC**

Hallmarks used 1814–31

large objects   **small objects**   **large objects**   **small objects**

Hallmarks used 1831–68

purity .950   **800**

hallmark large objects   **small objects**

large .900 objects   .800   small .900 objects   .800

Hallmarks used from 1942 onwards

large .925 objects   .835   small .925 objects   .835

DENMARK

Danish silver was marked with a city or town mark from the 17th century. From the late 17th century silver had four marks: town mark, assayer's mark (usually his initials in a square or oval cartouche), mark of the month (sign of the zodiac) and maker's mark. Copenhagen's mark usually incorporates the date. From 1888 Danish silver of a purity of .826 was stamped with an official mark showing the three towers of Copenhagen in an oval and the last two numbers of the year the piece was assayed.

Copenhagen The three towers of Copenhagen in an oval shield with date below were used between the early 17th and the 19th centuries. Usually only the last two numbers of the date appear after 1771. Only the last number appears between 1801-9.

1762   1799

1808   1850   1859

Aalborg Three towers in oval shield, sometimes with date, used between the mid-17th and the 19th centuries. Mark becomes more stylized in 19thC.

1800

Aarhus Similar mark used during 18th and 19th centuries. Name in full in rectangle also used.

18thC 19thC

Odense. Similar mark with or without date in shield of varying shape found between the 17th and 19th centuries. Name in full also used.

Viborg Two marks used from 17th to 18th century. Name in full used in 19th century.

18thC   19thC

Month marks
Zodiacal symbols used to indicate month of manufacture.

Hallmark since 1888

(.826 purity)

FRANCE

Most French silver has four marks: maker's mark, community or warden's mark, charge mark and discharge mark.

From the early 16th century silver objects made in Paris were stamped with crowned letters by the wardens of the silversmiths' guild – *La Maison Commune* – who were responsible for maintaining the purity of silver. The letters changed annually with each warden; some letters such as *J* and *U* were omitted.

1697–1717	C – Z (no J or U)	1764–84	A – U (no J)
1717–39	A – Z (no J or U)	1784–89	P (in various
1740–63	A – Z (no J or U)		sizes)

Examples of community marks of the Paris *maison commune*

A similar crowned letter *P* mark in various styles was used from 1784.

Charge and Discharge marks

When silver was assayed (usually in parts) it was marked with a charge mark. This showed that the piece was of the required standard and that duty was owed on the item. City charge marks were usually a letter – the letter for Paris was *A* – and their changing style can help with dating, although the marks are easily confused with some community marks used (see above). In the smaller provincial centres, a charge mark was often the town's arms or initials.

When the tax owed was paid to the tax farmer the piece was stamped with a discharge mark. Discharge marks also varied according to the region and often differ according to the size of the article.

This system of marking was abolished in 1791, in the aftermath of the 1789 French Revolution. Control over the standard of silver was re-established in 1797. Tax was collected by the State from this date on, and silver was marked with a more uniform system.

City Letter Charge Marks

A	Paris	P	Dijon
B	Rouen	Q	Perpignan
C	Caen	R	Orleans
D	Lyon	S	Reims
E	Tours	T	Nantes
F	Angers	V	Troyes
G	Poitiers	W	Lille
H	La Rochelle	X	Amiens
I	Limoges	Y	Bourges
K	Bordeaux	Z	Grenoble
L	Bayonne	&	Aix
M	Toulouse	AA	Metz
N	Montpellier	CC	Besancon
O	Riom	9	Rennes

(See individual city entries on following pages for facsimiles of city charge marks.)

Paris

Charge marks

1684–7

charge discharge

1687–91

charge discharge

1691–8

charge discharge

1697–1703

charge discharge

1704–12

charge discharge

1713–17

charge discharge charge discharge

1717–22

charge discharge

1722–7

charge discharge

1727–32

charge discharge

1732–8
charge   discharge

1738–44   charge   discharge

1744–50   charge   discharge

1750–6   charge   discharge

1756–62
charge   discharge

1762–8
charge   discharge

1769–75
charge   discharge

54 EUROPEAN SILVER MARKS

1775–81
charge

discharge

1781–9
charge

discharge

1789

charge

discharge

Regional Marks

Aix

1750 charge

1774–80
charge

discharge

charge

discharge

1780–90
charge

discharge

1780–91
charge

discharge

1780 community

Amien

1737–9
community

1764–74
charge

1762–8
discharge

1768–74
community

1784–91
community

Angers Letter *H* surmounted by crown used from 1716 to 1771. Word *ANGERS* appears in 1748, 1750, 1754. From 1774–1783 word *ANGERS* appears with letter.

1768–74
charge

1734–41
discharge

1716
community

1774

1784/9

Bordeaux Letter *K* in various styles, surmounted by a crown used from 17th century until 1789. Various discharge marks used. Letters *BOR* with date letter appear in most community marks between the 17th century and the early 18th century when it is replaced by the letter *B* and date letter.

1691–8 charge

1691–8 community

1689–1703 charge

1698–1703 community

1780–9
charge

discharge

1780–9
charge

discharge

1780
community

Dijon Letter *P* in various styles used between the late 17th and late 18th centuries. Discharge marks vary.

1691–8	c.1750	1756–9
charge	discharge	charge

1775–80	discharge	1780–91	discharge
charge		charge	

Grenoble Similar marks used between 1600–1760. Last two numbers of date used from *c.*1784.

community marks

| 1716–18 | 1741 | 1784–9 |

Lille Similar mark or date letter surmounted by a crown used in 18th century.

| 1750 | 1775 | 1770 |

Lyons Letter *D* in various styles used between the 17th century and the 1780s. Community mark shows lion rampant surmounted by crown with date letter from 1712–77. Later marks vary.

| 1775–80 | | 1780–91 | |

1780–91		1776
charge	discharge	community

Metz Shield with date letter used in mid-18th century. *AA* or *M* used during late 18th century.

1774–80 charge	discharge	mid-18thC community

1780–91 charge	discharge

Montpellier Letters *MP* intertwined or letter *N* used for charge mark during 18th century. Date letter surmounted by a crown above letters *MPL* used as community mark from 1709–82.

1709 community	1774–80 charge	discharge

1780–9 charge	discharge	18thC

Nancy Similar mark used throughout 18th century.

c.1790	late 18thC

Nantes Letter *T* used as charge mark until mid-18th century when word *NANTES* appears in full within a shield.

1744 charge	1746 discharge	1762–9 charge	1772 community

Orleans Letter *R* used as a charge mark from 1732 until *c.*1780. Various community marks used.

early 18thC community	1751–62 charge	discharge

Poitiers Three *P*s and a date letter used as a community mark during 18th century. Letter *G* surmounted by a crown in various styles used as charge mark between the 17th and late 18th centuries.

1744 community 1774–80 charge discharge

Reims Letter *S* used as charge mark between *c.*1768 and the late-18th century. Various community marks used.

*c.*1750 1768–74 charge discharge

community 1768–74   1784–91

Rennes Number *9* in various styles used as charge mark between the late 17th century and late 18th century. Community marks show letter surmounted by a crown.

1721 discharge   1725 community 1754–6 community

1756–62 charge 1780–9 charge   discharge

Riom Letter *O* used as charge mark during 18th century. Community marks vary.

1775–80 community 1780–9 charge discharge

La Rochelle Letters *H* or *LR* intertwined used as a charge mark. Various community marks used.

1774–80
charge discharge charge discharge

18thC community

Rouen Letter *B* surmounted by crown used as charge mark from late 17th century. Letter surmounted by crown used as community mark.

1774–80 charge   discharge

18thC community

Strasbourg Similar marks showing shield surmounted with *fleur-de-lys* and number *13* used between the mid-17th century and 1796. Sometimes a crown surmounts the number.

1725   1750–96   1752 date mark   1796

Toulouse Letter *M* used as charge mark from 16th century. Letters *TOL* surmounting a date letter in a shield used as a community mark between the late 17th and the late 18th centuries.

1768–74 charge   1776 community   1780–9 charge   discharge

Tours Letter *E* surmounted by crown used as charge mark from early 18th century. Community marks show various crowned letters.

1739 community   1768–74 charge   1774–80 charge   discharge

1780–9 discharge marks

Later French Marks

1793–4

1795–7

1797

1798

1798–1809

1809–19

1819–38

1879 onwards

GERMANY

Silver was marked in Germany from the 15th century. German silver submitted for assay was marked to indicate its maker and town of origin. Town marks changed slightly over the centuries and can help with dating. The towns of Nuremberg, Königsberg and Dresden also had date letter systems. There was no consistent purity guarantee for German silver before 1884. Since then, purity has been indicated in numbers, expressed as thousandths, and the crown and crescent mark of Germany denotes a purity of at least .800.

Augsburg Variations
on mark used between
16th century and 1800.

1767/9

Berlin Variations on bear mark used between the late
17th and 19th centuries. Date letter appears after *c.*1750.

early 18thC

19thC

Cologne Similar marks used between the 17th and late
18th centuries.

late 17thC

late 18thC

Dantzig Variations on
mark used between the16th
and 18th centuries.

17th/18thC

Dresden Variations on these marks used from between
the 18th century and the mid-19th century. The word
DRESDEN sometimes appears in full on later pieces.

early 18thC

late 18thC

19thC

Date letters found on Dresden silver of the 18th to 19th
century.

Düsseldorf Anchor mark only used during 17th and
18th century. Anchor with lion, sometimes surmounted
by a number *12* or *13*, used during 18th century.

18thC

Essen Similar mark
used from 17th to
18th century.

17th/18thC

Frankfurt Similar mark used between the 16th and the late 18th centuries.

17th/18thC   mid-18thC

Hamburg Similar mark on shield of varying background used between the 16th and 19th centuries.

17th/18thC

Hanover Similar mark with last two numbers of date used from 2nd half of 17th century to mid-18th century.

mid-18thC

Königsberg Similar mark used between the late 17th and mid-19th centuries.

early 18thC   mid-18thC   1815

date letters

1712	a	1714	C	1715	c	1740	D
1742	F	1747	L	1754	S	1761	Z
1766	P	1773	M	1784	✿	1788	B
1818	A.	1843	A				

Leipzig Letter *L* used between the 16th and 17th centuries. Crossed swords with letter *L* and number *12* used between the 17th and 18th centuries.

17thC L   17th/18thC

Lubeck Similar mark used between the 16th and 18th centuries.

18thC

Luneburg Similar mark with shield of varying shape used between the early 16th and the 17th centuries. Crescent moon with number *12* in circle used in early 19th century.

mid-17thC   early 19thC

Magdeburg Castle of varying design used between the early 17th and the 18th centuries.

early 18thC

Mannheim Similar marks recorded during 18th century.

early 18thC   late 18thC

Munich Similar mark used from late 17th century. Date appears with figure between 1742 and 1795.

18thC

           mid-18thC

Nuremberg

late 18thC	early 19thC	date letters	
N	**N**	1766–9 **A**	1769–73 **B**
1773–6 **C**	1776–80 **D**	1780–3 **E**	1783–7 **F**
1787–90 **G**	1790–4 **H**	1794–7 **I**	1797–1800 **K**

19thC

b   **6**   **f**   **8**

Prussia 1809

Regensburg 18thC

Strasburg Similar mark
used between the 16th and
mid-17th centuries.

mid-17thC

Stuttgart Similar mark with horse used between late
16th to 19th century. Date letter appears from late 18th
century. Other marks also found in 19th century.

late 17thC   early 18thC   late 18thC   19thC

Uberlingen Similar mark used between the 16th and
18th centuries.

18thC

Ulm Similar mark on shield of varying shape used
between the 16th and 18th centuries.

17thC   early 18thC   18thC

Purity mark for
German silver
made after 1888

ITALY

There was no uniform system of marking until 1810
when, under decree of Emperor Napoleon, assay offices
were established in Milan, Venice, Ancona, Verona and
Brescia. Prior to this, many towns and territorial states
adopted their own hallmarks, often stamped by the
guilds. From 1873 uniform hallmarking was adopted
throughout the country. Purity was not obligatory but
marks denoting purities of .950, .900 and .800 were
used. New standards of .925 and .800 were introduced
in 1935.

Florence

17th–18thC   18thC

Genoa Similar mark used between the 16th and 18th centuries.

18thC

Milan 1810

Naples Marks showing letters *NAP* sometimes surmounted by a crown used between the 15th and mid-18th centuries. Last three numbers of date sometimes appear.

1716 1720

Palerma 18thC

Rome Crossed keys mark used between the 17th century and late 18th century.

late 17thC   late 18thC

Hallmarks of purity
used from early
18th century

Turin Similar mark used in 18th and 19th century. 1809

Venice Marks very varied, some 19th century marks include date.

17th–18thC   1805   1810–15

Assay marks in Genoa, Appenines and Montenotte

.950   .900   .800

Modern silver marks (after 1934)

NETHERLANDS

From the mid-17th century silver was marked with maker's mark, date letter, town mark, assayer's mark and a hallmark showing the crowned lion which guaranteed the purity of .875. New purity standards of .934 and .833 were used between 1806–10. The Netherlands adopted French marking systems from 1811 until 1953.

Amsterdam

mid-17thC   early 18thC

Arnhem Similar mark used from 17th to 18th century. Letters *HOLS* also sometimes appears.

18thC

den Bosch   late 18thC

Dortrecht Various marks used in 18th century.

18thC

Gouda 17thC

Maestricht 18thC

Rotterdam City arms or lion rampant surmounted by crown used between the 17th and 18th centuries.

18thC

Utrecht 17thC

Zwolle Crossed shield appears in mark between the early 17th and early 19th centuries.

late 18thC-early 19thC

Assay Office Marks

Amsterdam	Arnhem	Den Bosch	Delft

Dortrecht	Gouda	The Hague	Rotterdam

Utrecht	Zwolle

Purity marks from 1810–1814

large .950   .800   small .800

Purity marks from 1814–1953

large .934   .833   small .833

Tax marks

Date letters from 1814–1962

1814	1834	1835	1859
1860	1884	1885	1909
1910	1934	1935	

| 1944 - Nov 1945 | Nov 1945 - 1947 | 1948 - July | July - 1949 |

Marks on silver made after 1953

large .925   .835   small .835   .800

NORWAY

Early Norwegian marks usually comprised a city mark, the date (or a letter designating the year). From the mid-17th century to the mid-18th century, silver production was controlled by the king and the guilds were abolished. From 1766 silver was marked with a monthly mark, expressed either as a fraction or as a sign of the zodiac. A city mark, with seven balls and the date, was used from 1781 in Bergen. Many date marks show only the last two numbers of the date.

Bergen Letter *B* surmounted by crown in shield of varying shape used from 1580 to 1686. From 1740 to 1802, city gate, sometimes with date, used. Mark became increasingly stylized during 19th century. Mid-century mark shows only seven balls.

1767   1802   1856

Oslo 1647

Tronheim Similar flower mark used between the early 18th and the mid-19th centuries.

1744   1746   1860

Date marks

During the 19th century date marks sometimes appear in full or are shown by last two numbers of the year.

1802   1832   1843

Monthly marks

From 1740–65 monthly marks were shown as signs of the zodiac. From 1766–1820 fractions of twelve showed the month.

Dec 21 - Jan 21   Jan 21 - Feb 18   Feb 18 - March 20

March 20 - April 20	April 20 - May 21	May 22 - June 21
June 21 - July 22	July 22 - Aug 21	Aug 21 - Sept 23
Sept 23 - Oct 23	Oct 23 - Nov 22	Nov 22 - Dec 21

Purity marks

Norway (since 1893) purity .830-.925-

PORTUGAL

Before 1881 Portuguese silver was marked with a maker's mark and a town mark which guaranteed a purity of .958. Town marks usually consisted of the first letter of the town concerned within a shield of varying form. State hallmarking was introduced in 1881 and purity standards of .916 and .833 became obligatory from 1886. New hallmarking systems were introduced in 1938 and continue to this day:

Braga Similar mark used between the late 17th and late 18th centuries.
late 18thC

Coimbra Similar mark used between the late 17th and late 18th centuries.
late 18thC

Evora Letter *E* in various styles used between first half of the 18th century and the early 19th century.
1738

Faro
19thC

Guimaraes Letter *G* in shield of varying shape used between the mid-18th and mid-19th centuries.
mid-18thC

Lisbon Letter *L* used in shield of varying shape between the late 17th and late 19th centuries.

late 17thC   early 18thC   early 19thC

Oporto Letter *P* used in shield of varying shape between the late 17th and late 19th centuries.

late 17thC   early 18thC   1791–1810   1836–43

Purity marks used from 1886–1888

Lisbon   Oporto

Purity marks from 1886–1938

Lisbon - large .916   .833 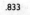   Oporto - large .916   833

small .916   .833   small .916   .833

Marks used from 1938

Lisbon   Oporto

RUSSIA

In Moscow silver had been marked from 1613. The first mark showed a two-headed eagle. In 1684 the eagle was replaced with a purity mark and date mark inside a circle. The eagle returned to use from 1700–10 and carried a sceptre and orb.

Assay offices were established in Moscow and St Petersburg during the first half of the 18th century. Throughout the 18th and 19th centuries silver made in Moscow or St Petersburg was marked by the maker, the guild, and the assay office where it was stamped with the mark of the assayer and the office.

From 1729 in Moscow, the date was stamped separately and the assayer's initials were marked beneath the eagle. From 1733 the word *MOCKBA* apppeared under the eagle. After 1741 a new mark, showing St George killing the dragon was introduced.

Provincial silver was marked with the town mark, maker's mark and a mark of purity in figures in a rectangular shield. A comprehensive system of marking was introduced in 1891; this included the initials of the assayer and a woman's head.

Moscow

1696   1702   1728

1731   1741

1782   1880

Assayers' marks

1841   1875–80   1890–5

Astrakhan Similar mark used in shield of varying shape between the 18th and 19th centuries.

1828

Kiev Name in full appears during 18th century. New mark, sometimes incorporating date, introduced in early 19th century.

1735–74   1828–87   1848–65   1825–47

Novgorod

1717–32 1851–62

Similar mark used from 1738–1862.

1864

Odessa Anchor mark used during 19th century.

1843–4   19thC

Petrograd (St Petersburg) City arms mark used with date until 1825, after which date no longer appeared.

1700–30 1730–40 1742

Vladimir Similar mark used in shield of varying shape with or without date between the mid-18th and mid-19th centuries.

1763–78 1863

Marks of purity on Russian silver from 1882

National mark from 1896

National mark from 1908–1917

National mark from 1927–1958

SPAIN

From the 16th century, silver was marked with a maker's mark and a town mark. According to royal decree only silver of a purity of .930 was admissable. Date marks began to be used in certain towns at the end of the 18th century. Two lower standards were established in 1881, and silver could be assayed on request. From 1934 items were stamped with maker's mark and mark of purity.

Barcelona Letters *BA*, 18thC
or *BAR* used between early
17th and 18th centuries.

Cordoba Lion of varying 19thC
styles, sometimes with letters
COR, used between 15th and
19th centuries.

Gérona 1786

Madrid 1797

Toledo Letter *T* or 17thC
TOL appears in mark
from 16th century.

Assay marks after 1881

.750 .916

SWEDEN

By the 16th century, Swedish silver was marked with both a maker's and a town mark. Date letters were introduced during the late 17th century in Stockholm. During the mid-18th century the State controlled the purity of silver objects. A comprehensive date letter system was adopted throughout Sweden and Finland from 1758. From 1860 different assay offices adopted letter marks.

Stockholm Crown mark used from *c.*1690–*c.*1715, when it was replaced by crowned head until *c.*1850.

late 17th–early 18thC   18th/19thC

Date letters used on Stockholm silver

A	1689	*A*	1713	*a*	1737
B	1690	*B*	1714	*b*	1738
C	1691	*C*	1715	*c*	1739
D	1692	*D*	1716	*d*	1740
E	1693	*E*	1717	*e*	1741
F	1694	*F*	1718	*f*	1742
G	1695	*G*	1719	*g*	1743
H	1696	*H*	1720	*h*	1744
I	1697	*I*	1721	*i*	1745
K	1698	*K*	1722	*k*	1746
L	1699	*L*	1723	*l*	1747
M	1700	*M*	1724	*m*	1748
N	1701	*N*	1725	*n*	1749
O	1702	*O*	1726	*o*	1750
P	1703	*P*	1727	*p*	1751
Q	1704	*Q*	1728	*q*	1752
R	1705	*R*	1729	*r*	1753
S	1706	*S*	1730	*s*	1754
T	1707	*T*	1731	*t*	1755
U	1708	*V*	1732	*u*	1756
V	1709	*W*	1733	*v*	1757
X	1710	*X*	1734	*w*	1758
Y	1711	*Y*	1735		
Z	1712	*Z*	1736		

Kalmar

18thC

Malmo

18thC

Orebro

18thC   19thC

City marks from 1912
From 1912 town marks were usually formed from the town's initial letter.

Town	Mark	Town	Mark	Town	Mark	Town	Mark
Ahus	Ⓐ	Gafle	Ⓖ	Karlstad	Ⓒ	Malmo	Ⓜ
Nora	Ⓝ	Sala	Ⓢ	Ystad	Ⓨ		𝕃

Date letters

A-Z 1759-82		Q2	1798	F4	1836
A	1759	R2	1799	G4	1837
B	1760	S2	1800	H4	1838
C	1761	T2	1801	I4	1839
D	1762	U2	1802	K4	1840
E	1763	V2	1803	L4	1841
F	1764	X2	1804	M4	1842
G	1765	Y2	1805	N4	1843
H	1766	Z2	1806	O4	1844
I	1767			P4	1845
K	1768	A3-Z3 1807-30		Q4	1846
L	1769	A3	1807	R4	1847
M	1770	B3	1808	S4	1848
N	1771	C3	1809	T4	1849
O	1772	D3	1810	U4	1850
P	1773	E3	1811	V4	1851
Q	1774	F3	1812	X4	1852
R	1775	G3	1813	Y4	1853
S	1776	H3	1814	Z4	1854
T	1777	I3	1815		
U	1778	K3	1816	A5-Z5 1855-78	
V	1779	L3	1817	A5	1855
X	1780	M3	1818	B5	1856
Y	1781	N3	1819	C5	1857
Z	1782	O3	1820	D5	1858
		P3	1821	E5	1859
A2-Z2 1783-1806		Q3	1822	F5	1860
A2	1783	R3	1823	G5	1861
B2	1784	S3	1824	H5	1862
C2	1785	T3	1825	I5	1863
D2	1786	U3	1826	K5	1864
E2	1787	V3	1827	L5	1865
F2	1788	X3	1828	M5	1866
G2	1789	Y3	1829	N5	1867
H2	1790	Z3	1830	O5	1868
I2	1791			P5	1869
K2	1792	A4-Z4 1831-1854		Q5	1870
L2	1793	A4	1831	R5	1871
M2	1794	B4	1832	S5	1872
N2	1795	C4	1833	T5	1873
O2	1796	D4	1834	U5	1874
P2	1797	E4	1835	V5	1875

X5	1876	F7	1908	Q8	1942
Y5	1877	G7	1909	R8	1943
Z5	1878	H7	1910	S8	1944
		I7	1911	T8	1945
A6-Z6 1879-1902		K7	1912	U8	1946
A6	1879	L7	1913	V8	1947
B6	1880	M7	1914	X8	1948
C6	1881	N7	1915	Y8	1949
D6	1882	O7	1916	Z8	1950
E6	1883	P7	1917		
F6	1884	Q7	1918	A9 -Z9 1951-74	
G6	1885	R7	1919	A9	1951
H6	1886	S7	1920	B9	1952
I6	1887	T7	1921	C9	1953
K6	1888	U7	1922	D9	1954
L6	1889	V7	1923	E9	1955
M6	1890	X7	1924	F9	1956
N6	1891	Y7	1925	G9	1957
O6	1892	Z7	1926	H9	1958
P6	1893			I9	1959
Q6	1894	A8-Z8 1927-50		K9	1960
R6	1895	A8	1927	L9	1961
S6	1896	B8	1928	M9	1962
T6	1897	C8	1929	N9	1963
U6	1898	D8	1930	O9	1964
V6	1899	E8	1931	P9	1965
X6	1900	F8	1932	Q9	1966
Y6	1901	G8	1933	R9	1967
Z6	1902	H8	1934	S9	1968
		I8	1935	T9	1969
A7-Z7 1903-26		K8	1936	U9	1970
A7	1903	L8	1937	V9	1971
B7	1904	M8	1938	X9	1972
C7	1905	N8	1939	Y9	1973
D7	1906	O8	1940	Z9	1974
E7	1907	P8	1941		

SWITZERLAND

The standards of purity were regulated in Zurich, Lucerne and Basel from the mid-16th century. Each canton adopted its own mark, usually a pictorial symbol with or without an intitial. Uniform purity in five standards – .935, .925, .900, .875 and 800 – was adopted from 1848. Uniform marks were adopted from 1882.

Geneva Similar mark used between the 17th and late 18th centuries.

17thC

1770

19thC

Lausanne 18thC

Luzern Similar mark with shield of varying shape used from *c.*1630–*c.*1760.

1701   1750

Neuville Similar mark with varying shield shape used between the late 16th and late 18th centuries.

1730   1752

Vevey Similar mark with variations used between 16th and 18th centuries. 18thC

Zurich Letter *Z* in shield used between the 16th and 18th centuries. 18thC

Marks used from 1882–1934
large .875 .800

U.S.A.

American makers marked their wares with their name or initials (*see pp162-5*) but there was no uniform regulation of silver purity, nor any comprehensive system of date or town marking. Although American marks are scant, cities such as New York and Boston had official societies, similar to the system of guilds which presided over European silversmiths; occasionally the place of origin is marked in full alongside the maker's mark.

Modern silver produced in the USA should be marked with the maker's name and numbers indicating the purity. The word STERLING appears on silver of .925 purity.

CANADA

From 1700–63, when Canada was under French rule, marks were similar to those used in France. Makers used their initials with a *fleur-de-lys* or crown, or star. The word *MONTREAL* or *QUEBEC* was sometimes marked on pieces made in these provinces. *H* or *HX* or *XNS* may be seen on pieces made in Halifax, Nova Scotia, and *ST J* or *NB* for St John, New Brunswick. From *c.*1800 Canadian marks copied those used in England. After 1898 date letters followed the London sequence. Modern Canadian-made silver of .925 purity may be marked with the national mark – a lion's head inside a letter *C*.

Canadian date letters

1898	a	1899	b	1900	C	1901	d
1902	d	1903	e	1925	k	1926	l
1927	m	1928	n	1929	o	1930	p
1931	q	1932	ñ	1934	s
1935	j	1936	A	1937	B	1938	C
1939	D	1940	E	1941	F	1942	G
1943	H

imitations of English marks   late 18thC

METHODS OF MANUFACTURE

Wrought silver can be produced in one of three ways: casting, rolling or raising. Casting or moulding involves the pouring of molten silver into sand moulds. The process was used mainly for the production of candlesticks. Cuttlefish moulds were sometimes used for the casting of jewelry and smaller silver objects. In the rolling process, an ingot of silver is beaten into sheet form, rolled into cylinders and the edges seamed together to create a tube. By letting in a base, simple cups and vessels can be made. With increasing sophistication the process became used for more elaborate hollow wares. Some pieces, such as candlesticks, required strengthening or stabilizing and were often "loaded" or "filled". This process, which involved fixing an iron rod inside the body using pitch or plaster, had the advantage of being significantly cheaper than casting. With raising, the metal was beaten out with a hammer, a hardening process called annealing. The piece was then heated to realign the structure of the atoms, thus restoring it to a state to withstand more beating, and so on, until the required shape was achieved.

METHODS OF DECORATION

The methods of decorating silver fall into three broad types: cast and applied, *repoussé* and engraved.

CAST AND APPLIED

Applied decoration refers to any decoration made separately and added, rather than integral to the form, and includes beading (a decorative border of tight beads).

A French covered bowl, c.1820, with applied decoration
and beaded border

Strapwork and cut-card work

Strapwork, probably brought to England by Huguenot craftsmen, consisted of interlacing straps or bands of ornament. These were originally engraved but, by the end of the 17th century, were cast and applied in a more elaborate form.

A two-handled cup and cover, c.1724, with strapwork panels and cut-card flutes

Cut-card decoration

During the late 17th century a more sophisticated version of strapwork, called cut-card work (whereby formalized leaves were applied to the surface in a decorative pattern), became fashionable. In much the same way as a pastry cook decorates a pie, so the silversmith cut straps and other shapes from silver and applied them with heat. As the period progressed, these too became chased and further decorated.

REPOUSSÉ

Repoussé means "pushed out", and is a combination of chasing and embossing which involves chasing the embossed metal in order to refine the design.

An 18thC jug with high-quality chased decoration

Chasing

A form of decoration worked with a hammer and punches, without cutting or carving the metal. Some examples of chasing are so fine they may be mistaken for engraving, of which chasing is almost the exact opposite. Chasing in high relief was popular during the late 17th century but its popularity subsided when plainer silver became fashionable during the early-18th century. However, the vogue for chased silver returned to great heights during the rococo period.

Flat chasing

A variation of the chasing process whereby the decoration appears in low relief. The technique is best exemplified in early *chinoiserie* style silverwares.

A late 17thC tankard decorated with flat-chased *chinoiserie* work

Embossing

Embossing is a form of relief decoration worked into the silver with a hammer or punch, leaving a raised pattern. Embossing can be done in two ways. The craftsman may work from the inside out, resting the piece on a sandbag (a leather pillow filled with sand), which is pliant enough to withstand the shape he is creating but firm enough to maintain the form. Alternatively, the piece may be worked in reverse, the inside being filled with pitch, which again is sufficiently pliant to allow indentation without the piece collapsing entirely.

Because of the way the design is created, embossed patterns are visible on the reverse of the piece. Once the general decoration has been created, details are applied, such as the veins of a leaf or fur of an animal. This is also a type of embossing, in that a hammer and punch are used and the effect is visible on the reverse.

ENGRAVING

Engraved decoration is incised into the surface of the metal. Coats of arms, presentation inscriptions and other marks of ownership were engraved on silverware entirely by hand, without using a hammer. Engraving is not visible on the reverse.

A Dutch beaker, c.1660, with elaborate engraved decoration

A salver with bright-cut decoration, c.1780

Bright-cut engraving

A type of decorative effect achieved by engraving a faceted design that stands out sharply. It was particularly popular during the late 18th and early 19th centuries. The method is very effective when used to create ribbons and bands of swags and festoons. Bright-cut work remained fashionable until well into the 19th century; Hester Bateman (*see p.107*) was one of its best known exponents.

A baluster vase, c.1910 with a planished (hammered) surface

SURFACE TREATMENTS

Planishing (hammering)

A significant feature of Arts and Crafts silver is the hand-beaten or planished surface, an effect not fashionable before that period. When a piece is raised, it is beaten with a hammer while being held against an anvil or fixed "head". The first series of hammerings are applied with an implement of a certain convex surface and, as work continues, hammers with a progressively lesser degree of convexity are used, until the final surface, which shows no dents, is achieved with a virtually flat hammer. Half-way through this process therefore, the surface has the dappled effect visible on the inside of many mid-18th century coffee pots, mugs and tankards of baluster form. The effect appealed to exponents of the Arts and Crafts movement, who perfected the difficult art of planishing a piece to a satisfactory degree of regularity.

Pouncing

This method involves the hammering of the surface of a piece with a punch, giving a dulled texture, yet with a sparkly effect. The surface then acted as a background to other decoration.

SILVER SUBSTITUTES

Electroplating

This technique involved the application of a layer of pure silver to a base metal (initially copper and nickel silver, later Britannia metal) using electrolysis. The method was developed as a commercial venture by George Elkington in Birmingham in c.1840 and its introduction coincided with a fashion for naturalistic designs not easily produced by other methods. EPBM and EPNS indicate electroplated Britannia metal and electroplated nickel silver respectively. A large amount of serviceable silverwares was produced using both materials and, though widely used today, neither is particularly collectable in their own right.

Electrotyping

Electrotyping is a sophisticated development of electroplating that facilitates the accurate imitation of solid objects. A plaster mould is taken of the original object, coated with plumbago (graphite), then subjected to electrolysis. The silver deposited evenly on the plumbago provides an exact imitation of the original mould. Like electroplating, electrotyping was introduced by Elkington & Co.

Close plating

A method of applying a layer of silver foil to steel, an early decorative process used by cutlers to protect steel knives (especially dessert knives) from staining.

Gilding

A method of applying a thin layer of gold to silver: a mixture of gold leaf and mercury was spread over the relevant area and heated until the mercury evaporated. Following the introduction of electroplating, fire gilding, which produced toxic mercury fumes, was outlawed.

(For Sheffield Plate see p168).

ARMORIALS AND CARTOUCHES

Since pride of ownership first began, people have inscribed their silver within a decorative frame or cartouche. The humblest inscriptions may only be initials, the grandest, coats of arms and crests, but the type of shield and the style of cartouche can provide help in dating a piece that lacks a full set of marks, and may even indicate the original owner.

A full set of armorials can appear on larger pieces: this comprises a coat of arms surrounded by a cartouche, mantling, a motto and, for members of the peerage, a coronet and supporters.

Earl Duke Marquis

Viscount Baron

The colours of heraldry are represented by specific patterns of lines.

Blue
(azure)

Red
(gules)

Green
(vert)

Black (sable) Purple (purple)

Green and purple are uncommon. Silver is represented by a blank shield and gold by a shield filled with tiny dots. On smaller pieces of silver the family crest was often used.

There is an important distinction to be made between a crest and a coat of arms: a single crest may be shared by anything up to 20 families, whereas a coat of arms is traceable to a particular family or even a particular man and wife, which adds to the interest of the piece. Crests are sometimes coupled with mottoes. English crests have the motto below, whereas Scottish crests have the motto over the top.

Coats of arms are a good guide to dating. They are also used in Continental Europe, in styles that correspond to the English styles of each period. German arms often include helmets.

Inscriptions

Inscriptions that are contemporary with the piece add to its value. The most desirable are those that have a naval or military content, or are connected with institutions such as Lloyd's bank or the East India Company. Those that include the name of well-known people are also desirable. However, religious inscriptions (and items intended for religious, rather than for secular use) are not currently in great demand.

Inscriptions to civil engineers were common in the Victorian period.

Initials

Some pieces, particularly earlier ones, are engraved with three initials in a triangle. The upper, single initial usually represents that of the family surname, the lower two being the initials of the forenames of the husband and wife. Pieces thus engraved were often given as wedding presents. Initials can be helpful in tracing a coat of arms or a crest to a particular family or person.

Replacement and erasure of arms

When silver changed hands, the new owners sometimes erased the existing coat of arms and replaced it with their own, an act which can reduce the value of a piece (*see Fakes and Alterations pp172-9*).

BORDERS

Borders are an important decorative element of many different types of silverware. Their changing styles can give a useful indication of the date of an object. On early wares (1690-1700) gadroon borders were popular. At the beginning of the 18th century, simple moulded borders were applied to wares. Scrolled borders, sometimes referred to as "Chippendale" borders are found during the middle part of the 18th century. As the fashion for rococo styles took hold, elaborately-scrolled borders were sometimes pierced and often further embellished with cast and applied motifs; shells were especially prevalent. During the latter half of the 18th, century borders became more simple and delicate. Beaded borders and thread borders are often found on wares of this date. Heavier borders were favoured during the Regency period; gadroon borders were particularly popular at this time. Throughout the 19th century the borders of most earlier periods were resurrected, although their proportion in relation to the overall size of the piece was often increased.

1690-1700
gadroon border

1720-c.1730
applied moulded border

1730s-'40s
scrolled border

1740s-60
cast and applied motifs

1760s-'70s
gadroon border

1775-90
beaded border

1790s
thread border

c.1800-25
19thC-style gadroon border

c.1810-25
gadroon and shell border

c.1850-c.1895
shell and scroll border

SILVER STYLES

Style can prove a particularly useful guide to dating silver; recognizable shapes offer an immediate indication of the origin and period of a piece.

The majority of collectable silver available to us today dates from the mid-17th century and later. Earlier pieces rarely exist outside museums or churches and do not really concern us within this book. The earliest silver that most collectors are likely to encounter is Commonwealth silver (c.1655-1660), which was usually extremely plain and of basic construction. Decoration on such pieces was minimal, with lobed or ribbed borders, rather more for added strength than for appearance.

In reaction to the austerity of the Cromwellian era, the Restoration saw a revival in the popularity of display silver and an explosion of variety in design. King Charles II, returning from exile, brought with him Continental craftsmen whose new styles and manufacturing techniques altered the appearance of British silver. Fluid foliate shapes were used to decorate silverwares, and floral motifs and fruit were popular adornments.

The Revocation of the Edict of Nantes in 1685 brought thousands of French Protestants, or Huguenots, to Britain. Among them were many superb silversmiths with their own approach to manufacture and decoration. The raising of the silver standard in 1697 (see p9) brought further changes in style. Huguenot silversmiths were used to working with metal of this standard — the prevalent standard in France — and British silver styles fell heavily under their influence at this time. The Huguenots are particularly associated with lavishly ornamented silver and embellished their wares with engraved decoration derived from French pattern books; hitherto engraving had been little used by English silversmiths. The French craftsmen also introduced new items such as ewers, basins and tureens which, until this date, were not in general usage in Britain.

Silver dating from the early years of the 18th century, during and after the reign of Queen Anne (1702-14), was plainer in shape and form. Vessels were generally straight-sided, cylindrical and tapering, often faceted below beautifully domed tops; octagonal shapes were popular from c.1710. A variety of new wares were introduced during the 18th century; as tea, coffee and chocolate became fashionable drinks, teapots, coffee pots and chocolate pots became increasingly popular. Sauce boats, snuff boxes and racing-cups were also first made during this period.

There remained throughout much of the 18th century silver made to the plainest designs on the one hand, and on the other, in the extravagant and elaborate rococo style. This style originated in France and its popularization in Britain was largely due to the influence of successful Huguenot silversmiths, such as Pierre Platel and

Paul de Lamerie. Designs for high-style pieces were usually based on curvilinear shapes and often incorporate fanciful Chinese and Gothic decoration. Handles in the shape of a "C" scroll, shell motifs, and sinuous foliage are typical of this style, which reached the height of its popularity in the 1730s and '40s. Pieces with extreme rococo decoration are rare and expensive, but simpler wares of the period usually contain elements of the style.

The exuberant rococo style gave way to neo-classicism from the middle of the 18th century. The new style was inspired by growing interest in Greco-Roman art and architecture, following the excavations of Herculaneum and Pompeii, and was popularized in the designs of architect Robert Adam. Adam is known also to have worked closely with Boulton and Fothergill of Birmingham to design "Adam" silverware. During the neo-classical period, heavy gadroon edges were replaced with beading, and swirling tendrils became carefully tailored drapes. The emphasis was on grace, elegance and simplicity. Silver of this period often mirrors the oval shapes of Greek and Roman vases. Decorative motifs drawn from classical antiquity include swags, rams heads, laurel leaves and acanthus leaves, and are delicately refined. By the 1790s silver surfaces were often engraved in a new style known as "bright cut" (see p84).

Towards the end of the 18th century a new style evolved, based on increased knowledge and understanding of Greek, Roman and Egyptian antiquity. In England this new style is known as "Regency", in France it is termed "Empire". During this period, which lasted from c.1790-1830, the proportions of silverwares changed dramatically, often becoming massively heavy. Decorative motifs were also weightier and more sombre – among the most popular are lyres, lion's feet, masks and heavy beaded borders.

The French revival, which resurrected the naturalistic curvilinear forms of the rococo period, started in c.1827 and continued after the death of George IV in 1830. The rococo revival mingled the foliate forms of the early 18th century with the larger proportions of Regency style. Silverwares are often broad and low, with a strong horizontal emphasis and boldly applied decoration. As the 19th century progressed, designers increasingly relied on past styles. Gothic motifs had provided an undercurrent of inspiration throughout much of the 18th century, but during the 19th century the Gothic revival in particular found great favour with the sombre Victorian outlook, and is reflected in silverwares by decorative Gothic arches, pinnacles and spires decorated with crockets.

The Great Exhibition of 1851 revolutionized public access to domestic items in a fashionable style; new machinery and materials facilitated the mass-manufacture of exotic-looking pieces for a modest price. By the end of the 19th century, domestic silver was produced on a huge scale, whilst electroplated nickel silver and electro-plated Britannia metal fashioned in silver shapes had found a market in their own right. The silver standards could not, of course, alter, but designs became enormously varied. As the Middle and Far East caught the imagination of the English, Moorish and Islamic patterns were incorporated into those already existing, and it is not surprising that a movement should emerge in support of traditional hand crafting. Under the influence of this Arts and Crafts movement of the late 19th century, designs, particularly for furniture and silver, became sinuous and natural. It was also at this time that octagonal-sided wares, in true reproduction of the early 18th-century style became fashionable once again. Indeed, during the first 30 years of the 20th century, all earlier styles were faithfully reproduced, and apart from the severe undecorated lines of the Art Deco style, there was generally, little innovation in styles from that period.

Because of Ireland's political connections, Irish silver has, for the most part, had strong links with contemporary silver in England. Some exquisite early Celtic silver survives in Ireland, from between the 8th and 12th centuries. There is then a gap of four centuries, until the re-establishment of the Dublin Goldsmiths' Company. Until c.1720, Irish silver is similar in style to London silver, but may be more traditional in design than English silver of the period, which was already under the French Huguenot influence. During the 18th century, Ireland's largely absentee Anglo-Irish aristocracy tended to buy silver in London and to demand that any Irish-bought silver exhibit English characteristics. It was only with the development of a more purely Irish middle class that Irish silver was able to develop its own shapes.

Irish silver is sometimes of a lower quality than English silver, but frequently exhibits exquisite bright-cut work and unusual features, such as pointed handles. Ireland's Union with England introduced the English to the rich surface decoration popular in Ireland; this was a style that found an admiring audience in Regency and Victorian England. Though initially good for Ireland's flourishing silver trade, the Union ultimately destroyed it, as the Irish styles began to be copied in England. However, from the beginning of the 20th century a national style re-emerged, based on the historic Celtic forms that regained popularity after a Gaelic revival.

NOTE

The following pages show the principal styles popular in Britain, followed by selected European styles. Silver in the United States followed English silver, but usually of an earlier period, as styles took a while to cross the Atlantic. American silver became increasingly ornate from the Victorian period.

ILLUSTRATED SILVER STYLES

Most baskets incorporate pierced decoration which can be vulnerable to damage; condition is therefore important in assessing value. Few predate the mid-18th century. Early baskets are usually oval, some have side handles. Later ones are usually lighter in weight and have "swing" handles. Oblong and circular shaped baskets were made from the end of the 18th century. Hallmarks are usually found on the base, footrim or side.

c.1735 c.1740 c.1765

c.1775 c.1790 c.1805

c.1810 c.1815 c.1825

c.1832 c.1840 c.1860

c.1860 c.1870 c.1905

The Hague c.1775 France c.1825 Germany 20thC

c.1761

c.1805

c.1810

c.1844

c.1875

Paris c.1747

CANDELABRA
Most candelabra date from the mid-18th century onwards. The design of bases follows that of candlesticks of the same period (see below). Candelabra are rarer and considerably more sought-after than candlesticks. Most are hallmarked on the base and the branches should also be marked.

France c.1768

France c.1788

CANDLESTICKS
Candlesticks became taller and heavier throughout the 18th century, ranging from about 6in/15cm –11in/30cm. Hallmarks are most commonly found on the underside of the base of cast sticks, or on the side of the base of loaded ones (*see p81 for explanation of different methods of manufacture*); detachable sconces and nozzles should also be marked. Candlesticks nearly always come in pairs or larger sets and fall considerably in value when sold singly.

c.1666

c.1685

c.1691

c.1708

c.1713

c.1725   c.1738   c.1748   c.1750   c.1753

c.1755   c.1764   c.1770   c.1805   c.1810

c.1845   c.1875   France c.1744   Germany c.1805   Italy c.1770

CASTERS

Casters were used from the late 17th century onwards,
usually for dispensing sugar or pepper. Early examples
have straight sides and pierced covers; later in the century octagonal and baluster shapes were introduced and
some covers were unpierced (blind). Casters became
taller throughout the 18th century. Most are hallmarked
on the base or on the side; detachable covers should also
be marked.

c.1693   c.1700   c.1708

c.1723   c.1749   c.1761

c.1770   c.1785   c.1800   c.1855

c.1910   France early 18thC   Germany c.1790   Germany c.1800

COFFEE POTS AND CHOCOLATE POTS

Most coffee pots date from the early 18th century or later. They are usually taller than teapots to keep the spout above the sediment. Early coffee pots have side handles and a tapering cylindrical shape with high-domed lids. Later in the century lids were shallower, and baluster, vase-shaped, and oblong pots were popular. Marks should be scattered on the base or in a line on the side.

c.1702   c.1710   c.1713

c.1719   c.1734   c.1739

c.1767   c.1771   c.1790

c.1805 c.1810 c.1815

c.1829 c.1851 c.1870

Germany c.1760 France c.1774 Germany c.1820-40

CRUETS

Spices and flavourings were an important element in 18th-century cooking, and cruet frames, to contain the necessary bottles and casters on the table, became prevalent during the century. Cruets are very varied in form; many contain silver-mounted glass bottles. They are usually marked on the main stand as well as on the component parts.

c.1735 c.1770 c.1780

c.1788 c.1802 c.1813

c.1840

c.1860

France c.1765

Netherlands c.1777

Germany c.1794

ENTRÉE DISHES

Entrée dishes became popular from the 1770s onwards.
Until the 1830s most were oval or rectangular in shape.
Earlier examples are often shallower than those made
during the Regency period and later. Handles are usually detachable. Entrée dishes are usually sold in pairs and
marked with numbers or dots to identify their matching
lid. Hallmarks are usually in a straight line on the lid and
base.

c.1775

c.1790

c.1795

c.1810

c.1815

c.1820

c.1830

c.1835

c.1845

c.1880

France c.1820-40

France 20thC

EPERGNES AND CENTREPIECES

Epergnes were used from the middle of the 18th century to display fruit and sweetmeats on the table. Early examples consist of a large basket surrounded by four smaller containers or baskets. Later designs can have six or more baskets; most are highly elaborate. All the component parts of the epergne should be marked.

c.1750   c.1760   c.1770

c.1790   c.1790   c.1810

c.1860   c.1880   c.1910

Germany c.1761   Germany late 19thC

JUGS

Small jugs for milk or cream were uncommon during the early 18th century and usually resemble coffee pots of the period, with high domed lids. During the 1720s, small jugs without lids were introduced. Mid-century examples had three cast feet, scrolled handles and curvilinear rims. Later, plain pear-shapes with pedestal feet predominate. Jugs are usually marked on the underneath or on the body by the handle or spout.

c.1729   c.1730   c.1739

c.1745

c.1756

c.1765

c.1780

c.1795

c.1800

c.1800

c.1840

c.1894

France c.1740

France c.1756

France c.1772

France c.1778

France c.1810-20

Italy c.1815-25

SALTS

Salt was kept in pairs of salt cellars from the beginning of the 18th century. Trencher salts were among the earliest examples and are usually marked inside the bowl. By the mid-century most salts had three feet, sometimes decorated with a lion's head mask. During the neo-classical period oval salts with pedestal bases were made. Salts are most usually marked on the base; on circular shapes the marks will be scattered.

c.1592

c.1594

c.1629

1650-1700

c.1695

c.1707

c.1760

c.1761

c.1790

c.1800

c.1840

c.1850

c.1850

c.1855

c.1870

Netherlands c.1624

Switzerland c.1780

France c.1809-19

SALVERS AND WAITERS

Early salvers are often circular in shape with a central
foot. Armorials are usually the only surface decoration
before 1730. From c.1730 square shapes and increasingly
elaborate borders and surface decoration proliferated and
some salvers had three or four feet. Oval shapes were

popular from *c*.1785. Salvers measuring under 6in/15cm are termed waiters. Hallmarks are usually found on the surface of the tray before *c*.1720, or on the underside after that date.

c.1700   from side   c.1704

c.1713   c.1731   c.1737

c.1742   c.1795   c.1805

c.1825   c.1858   c.1875

c.1875   Italy/Spain early 17thC   Germany c.1732

SAUCE BOATS

The earliest sauce boats date from *c*.1715. Early examples are shallow with two handles and lips and a wavy rim. From *c*.1730 sauce boats became deeper with a single lip and central pedestal foot. Later examples often had three feet. Hallmarks are usually underneath in a straight line.

c.1717   c.1727   c.1737

c.1747   c.1790   c.1850

Switzerland c.1765   Netherlands c.1770   France c.1776

SPOONS

Early spoons had fig-shaped bowls and decorative finials,
sometimes modelled in the form of an apostle. By the
1680s the bowl became more ovoid with Rat-tail rib at
the back, and handles terminated in a trefid. During the
Queen Anne period the handles evolved in the dog's
nose form. Throughout the 18th century the bowl
became more pointed and the Hanoverian (sometimes
called Rat-tail) and Old English patterns predominated
for handles. During the 19th century, many new, sometimes highly elaborate, patterns were introduced, most of
which have continued to be produced ever since.

Apostle Spoon
15th-17thC

St Matthias   St James   St Jude
the Greater

St Matthew   St Andrew   St Simon

St Thomas   St John   St Peter

St James   St Philip   St Bartholomew
the Less

Hour glass

Fiddle thread and shell

Fiddle thread

Old English thread

Onslow

Old English

Rat-tail

Albany

Coburg

Beaded

Albert or Charlotte

Queen's

King's

c.1500   c.1585   c.1681   c.1709

TANKARDS

Most tankards date from *c.*1660–late 18th century.
Tankards differ from mugs in that they have lids,
although they follow a similar stylistic development.
Early examples are usually straight-sided; during the late
17th century chased decoration, cut-card work and
engraving were often used to embellish surfaces.
Tankards of the 18th century are usually plain, possibly
only ornamented with a coat of arms. Marks should be
found on the side of the body or base and on the lid.

c.1572   c.1661   c.1670   c.1678

c.1701   c.1723   c.1728   c.1731

c.1760   c.1776   c.1795   c.1850

c.1858-9   Germany c.1650   Germany c.1650   Baltic c.1670

TEAPOTS

Teapots were made from the early 18th century
onwards. Until *c.*1760 they are relatively small because
tea was expensive. The early pear-shaped form was
replaced from *c.*1730–*c.*1750 by the bullet shape. From
*c.*1770 drum-shaped and then oval teapots became fashionable. The oblong shape was introduced in the early
19th century. Marks are usually found on the base; lids
should also be marked.

c.1720

c.1724

c.1725

c.1750

c.1774

c.1790

c.1798

c.1810

c.1817

c.1828

c.1835

c.1850

c.1859

Denmark c.1743

France c.1819-25

TUREENS

Sauce tureens first appeared *c.*1760. Most have covers with a cut-out to accommodate the sauce ladle; some also have trays on which they stand. During the Adam period sauce tureens were decorated with beaded borders and classical motifs and have pedestal feet. Some later examples have four legs and were more heavily proportioned. Few sauce tureens were made after 1830. Marks are usually found on the underneath of the body and on the lid.

c.1771

c.1776

c.1790

c.1811   c.1820   c.1840

France c.1805   Germany c.1811   Russia c.1811

TWO-HANDLED CUPS

Early two-handled cups are termed caudle cups or porringers. Caudle was a drink traditionally given to women
after childbirth. Most have covers and are of a straight-
sided or bulbous shape. From the 18th century two-handled cups were used at banquets and as decorative pieces,
becoming taller with a pedestal foot. During the 19th
century the two-handled cup was a popular shape for
trophies; some were of large proportions and lavishly
ornamented. Marks should be found on the base, body
or handle and on the lid.

c.1686   c.1692   c.1702

c.1714   c.1735   c.1751

c.1774   c.1776   c.1808

c.1841 c.1860 Netherlands late 16thC

Germany
c.1600

Netherlands
c.1642

Germany
c.1750

Germany
c.1890

WINE FUNNELS

Wine funnels were made from *c*.1770 and used for decanting wine. They usually consist of either a conical bowl with a detachable spout, or a main bowl containing a liner with a perforated base. A piece of muslin was inserted in the base to strain the wine. Most were plain as they were purely functional objects. The complete hallmarks should be found on the bowl and the spout and inner bowl should also have marks.

c.1710 c.1790 c.1800

c.1815 c.1830

IMPORTANT BRITISH SILVERSMITHS

Among silversmiths there are a few names that stand out as being responsible for a consistently high standard of design, execution and decoration.

Charles Robert Ashbee (1863-1942)
An influential designer of early 20th century silver, Ashbee trained as an architect before becoming a leader of the Arts and Craft movement. He was a founder member of the Guild of Handicraft, which consisted of a circle of artist-craftsmen who sought to perpetuate medieval handcraftsmanship. Ashbee had no formal training as a silversmith but his early work was especially innovative. In 1909 Ashbee published *Modern English Silverwork* in which he expounded his theories on silver design.

Asprey & Co Ltd (c.1781-present day)
The company is believed to have been founded in 1781 in Mitcham, Surrey by William Asprey. By 1805 the firm had moved to London premises and was under the direction of Francis Kennedy. Early in the 19th century Kennedy was joined by Charles Asprey snr who by mid-century had left Kennedy and set up his own premises in New Bond Street. Throughout the 19th century and afterwards, Asprey was acclaimed as one of London's leading silver manufacturers and retailers.

Hester Bateman (1709-1794)
Hester Needham married John Bateman, a maker of gold watch chains, in 1732, and established a family silversmith business near the City of London. Early pieces were mainly flatwares; they later graduated to larger domestic objects. They produced vast quantities of attractive silverwares. Hester first registered her maker's mark in 1761, a year after her husband's death. However, her work is rarely found on pieces dated earlier than 1774 because during the intervening years she was occupied running the shop and co-ordinating commissions. After 1744 she appears to have concentrated on her own silversmithing, producing refined shapes with restrained decoration, often restricted to beading along the edges. Much

of Hester Bateman's early work was commissioned by other contemporary silversmiths, many of whom obliterated her mark with their own.

On her retirement in 1790, Bateman handed over the business to her sons, Peter and Jonathan. On Jonathan's death in 1791 his widow Ann entered a mark in conjunction with her brother-in-law. Her son, William, joined the partnership in 1800 and the three entered a joint mark. The mark of Peter and William Bateman was entered on Ann's retirement in 1805. Peter remained in control of the business until 1839, when he handed it down to his son, William (*see also p116*).

John Cafe (active 1740-1757)
Little is known of John Cafe (or possibly Case), other than that he registered his mark with Goldsmiths' in 1742 and specialized in the manufacture of candlesticks, chambersticks, snuffers and trays. His business was bankrupt in 1757 and was taken over by his brother William (*see also p119*).

The Courtauld family (active 1708-1807)
A prolific maker of domestic pieces, Augustine Courtauld was apprenticed to Simon Pantin in 1701 and registered his first mark in 1708. Samuel Courtauld (b.1720), the son of Augustine, married Louisa Perina Ogier in 1747. Little of his stronglyly rococo-style work survives. Louisa took over the family business on her husband's death in 1765. Her son Samuel also joined the firm and later emigrated to America (*see pp121-2*).

Christopher Dresser (1834-1904)
An important English designer and writer who was preoccupied with the need for good design and the importance of mechanization, Dresser designed revolutionary modern-style silverwares and electroplate for the firms of Elkington and Hukin & Heath from 1875-8. His designs are usually dictated by the function of the object, most are extremely simple and geometric in appearance; exposed rivets are a favourite motif.

Elkington & Co. (1801-65)
Elkington & Co. are renowned for their development of the electroplate process

which revolutionized the production of inexpensive silverware. The technique was first patented by the company in 1840. Later Elkington granted special licenses to other companies, such as the French firm Christofle, to produce their own electroplate. Elkington produced large quantities of useful household objects, many of which were used to equip hotels and clubs. Designs reflect a great variety of influences; Eastern and Italian Renaissance motifs recur frequently.

AF Andrew Fogelberg (1732-93)

Andrew Fogelberg came from Sweden and he was probably already trained when he arrived in London *c.*1770. He formed a partnership with Stephen Gilbert from 1780-93 (*see p127*), and is especially well-known for pieces in the popular neo-classical style. Fogelberg seems to have pioneered the application of decorative cameo-like medallions to his silverwares. Paul Storr (*see p112*) was apprenticed to Fogelberg.

RG Robert Garrard (active 1818)

In 1792 Robert Garrard joined the partnership established by George Wickes and Edward Wakelin (*see p112 and p151*), which then became known as Wakelin & Garrard. Wakelin passed the business to Garrard when he retired in 1802, and he in turn was succeeded by his three sons Robert (1793-1881), James and Sebastian. The firm has remained in Garrard's hands ever since and became the Crown Jewelers and Goldsmiths in 1830.

EG Eliza Godfrey (active 1741)

Eliza Godfrey was the most prolific and popular of the women silversmiths operating in the mid-18th century. Godfrey had been briefly married to Abraham Buteaux (*see p119*) and in 1741 was left widowed by Benjamin Godfrey (*see p129*). Between her marriages and after her second husband's death she registered marks, continuing the business with enormous success and producing such fine silverwares that she was eligible for Bateman's title of "the best woman silversmith of the 18th century". Her work tends to feature cast and chased work with intricate pierced fret-work in the rococo style.

The Hennell family

The Hennell family established a silver-making dynasty in the 18th century that continues today. The first David Hennell registered his mark in 1736. He was joined by his son Robert in 1763, who worked with him until 1797. Robert Hennell registered his mark in 1753. Robert was a pioneer of the neo-classical style, revived in England by the work of Robert Adam. Hennell is best-known for fine small silver, sweetmeat baskets, epergnes, salt cellars and cutlery. David and Robert Hennell entered their mark in 1768. Robert and Samuel Hennell registered a mark in 1802 (*see pp132-3*).

Archibald Knox (1854-1933)

Archibald Knox was born and educated on the Isle of Man. His observation of Celtic remains there is reflected in the Celtic motifs decorating his silverwares. He made silver and other metalwares for Liberty & Co. and was the most important of designers commissioned by Liberty to produce designs for the "Cymric" silverware range. Among his most sought-after silverwares are those embellished with coloured enamelling.

Paul de Lamerie (1688-1751)

A Huguenot, Paul de Lamerie was born in the Low Counties and came to England with his parents in 1689, after the Revocation of the Edict of Nantes. He served his apprenticeship with Pierre Platel in 1703 and registered his first mark in 1712. De Lamerie worked consistently in Britannia silver until 1732, even though it was no longer compulsory after 1720. He entered a sterling silver mark in 1732. In 1739 de Lamerie entered a third mark and moved his workshop to Gerrard Street where he died in 1751. Although other 18th century silversmiths equalled de Lamerie in skill, his work is by far the most popular and collectable today. His early wares were in the restrained Queen Anne style but his most popular and famous pieces, many of which were royal commissions, are in an elaborate and highly decorative rococo style. However, de Lamerie also produced large numbers of simpler, useful wares.

Pierre Platel (active 1699-1719)

Platel was a French Huguenot silversmith who became a member of the Goldsmiths' Company in 1699. His work typifies the elaborate rococo styles favoured by the English aristocracy, for which the Huguenot silversmiths were renowned. The Prince of Wales was one of his patrons. Among his most elaborate and celebrated works are a ewer and dish in the form of a helmet made in 1701 (now at Chatsworth House). Platel had several apprentices who became successful in their own right, the most celebrated was Paul de Lamerie (*see previous page*).

Omar Ramsden and Alwyn Carr (1873-1939)

Ramsden and Carr registered a joint mark in 1898. They were among the new generation of silversmiths who carried on the ideals of traditional hand-making techniques into the modern age of mass-production. Ramsden entered a Gothic-style mark when he set up on his own in 1918. He was greatly influenced by Celtic art and medieval influences are often reflected in his designs. His work commonly features a hammer-marked (planished) surface (*see pp81-5*) and he often applied a Latin signature in addition to his mark.

Rundell, Bridge & Rundell (1788-1842)

The firm was established by Philip Rundell (1743-1827) and became one of London's most successful makers. In 1788 Rundell formed a partnership with John Bridge (*see p118*) and they were joined by Edmund Waller Rundell in 1803. The company was patronized by the Royal family, and had warrants from both the Prince of Wales and Duke of York. In 1806 they were recorded as employing 1,000 workers. Many of their more important wares were made by specially commissioned independent silversmiths, such as Paul Storr and Benjamin Smith (*see below*). John Flaxman modelled figures for some of the enormous presentation pieces in which the company specialized. The firm also made good-quality less elaborate pieces.

Benjamin Smith (b.1764)

An important Regency silversmith, Benjamin Smith was one of the major suppliers of wares to Rundell & Bridge (*see previous page*). Many designs were very similar to those of Paul Storr (*see below*); Smith specialized in baskets and open-work. Before 1792 he formed a company known as Boulton & Smith, with his brother James, and Matthew Boulton of Birmingham. In 1801 a disagreement led to a new partnership between Boulton and James Smith. In 1802 Smith moved from Birmingham to Greenwich. He formed a partnership with Digby Scott, registering marks with him in 1802 and 1803. In 1807 Smith registered two marks alone. In partnership with James he registered another mark in 1809. Further marks were recorded in 1812, 1814, 1816 (with his son Benjamin jnr), and 1818. Smith had a reputation for being difficult to work with (*see also p118 and p147*).

Paul Storr (1771-1844)

Paul Storr is perhaps the most famous of early 19th-century silversmiths. Originally apprenticed to the Swedish-born plate worker, Andrew Fogelberg (*see p109*), he concentrated on the production of fine and elaborate presentation silver, some of it to royal commission. As one of the English silversmiths who interpreted the French Empire style in a less formal manner, Storr was instrumental in the development of the English Regency style. He opened his own shop in 1796. Between 1807 and 1819 he worked in association with Rundell and Bridge (*see previous page*), during which time he produced a wide range of wares, mainly in the ancient Roman or rococo styles. In 1822 Storr formed a partnership with John Mortimer that was to last until 1838. Unlike de Lamerie, Storr appears to have made little ordinary or plain silver.

George Wickes (1698-1761)

George Wickes was apprenticed to Simon Wastell on 2 December 1712 and registered his first two marks in 1722. Wickes had a line of distinguished clients: among his most famous commissions were the Pelham Gold Cup, made to designs by William Kent, *c.*1736, and a table service consisting of 170 pieces, made for the Earl of Leinster. Most of his work reflects the French rococo style, with asymmetrical curvilinear decorative motifs which were popular at the time.

OTHER BRITISH AND IRISH MAKERS
AND THEIR MARKS

Listed below is a selection of some of the other best-known British and Irish silversmiths from the 17th–early 20th century. London was by far the most popular centre for British silversmiths; the vast majority of recorded makers were active in and around the capital; therefore, unless otherwise stated, all the following makers may be assumed to have been London-based.

Knowledge of the working lives of most silversmiths is largely gleaned from the various assay offices and from records kept by the Worshipful Company of Silver & Goldsmiths. Before a silversmith could register a mark on his own he was obliged to serve as an apprentice to a "Master" (a qualified silversmith). After a specified time the apprentice was granted his freedom (i.e. he was no longer apprenticed) and was permitted to set up business on his own. Many silversmiths went on to become members of the Company of Gold & Silversmiths, a process known as "being clothed with the livery" or "liveried". Some then progressed to become part of the governing body, becoming members of court; then wardens. The head of the company was known as Prime Warden.

All gold and silversmiths (also known as plate-workers) were basically divided into two categories: largeworkers and smallworkers. Largeworkers, as the name suggests, made objects of a more substantial size such as baskets, dishes, tureens and large hollow wares. Candlestick makers and salvermakers were largeworkers. Smallworkers made small pieces such as vinaigrettes, wine-labels and match boxes. Bucklemakers, snuff box makers, spectacle makers and watch-case makers were all types of smallworker.

The following list gives details of the apprenticeship of recorded makers together with the dates of their marks and examples of them and, where appropriate, the types of wares for which they are best-known. Many silversmiths registered a variety of marks.

William Abdy Registered marks as a smallworker in 1763, 1767, 1769, 1779 and 1784. His son Thomas worked as his apprentice. Died 1790.

Robert Abercromby Marks registered in 1731, 1739 and 1740. Specialized in making salvers.

Robert Abercromby & George Hindmarsh Salver makers (*see above*). Registered mark in 1731.

George W. Adams London plateworker. Registered mark in 1840.

Stephen Adams & William Jury Smallworkers. Registered marks together *c.*1758 and 1759.

Charles Aldridge Apprenticed to his uncle, Edward Aldridge and to Edward Adle. Registered mark in partnership with Henry Green (*see below*) in 1775 and further marks in 1786 and 1789.

Charles Aldridge & Henry Green Plateworkers. Registered marks in 1775 (*see above*).

Edward Aldridge Registered marks in 1724 and 1739. Registered mark in partnership with John Stampe in 1753. In 1742 tried by the Goldsmiths' Company for counterfeiting marks but acquitted by the Jury (*see below*).

Edward Aldridge & John Stamper Recorded mark in 1753 (*see above and below*).

William Alexander Apprenticed to Isabella Archer in 1707 and made a freeman in 1716. Registered only mark as a largeworker in 1743. One of the most important chandelier makers of the mid-18th century.

Joseph Allen & Mordecai Fox Allen recorded his first mark in partnership with Fox in 1730 from St Swithin's Lane, and his second with him in 1739.

John Angell Son of John Angell snr and apprenticed to him in 1825. John Angell snr did not register mark but worked with brother Joseph. John Angell jnr registered mark in partnership with uncle, Joseph Angell, in 1831 (*see below*).

Joseph Angell Apprenticed to Henry Nutting in 1796. Two marks registered in 1811 and 1824 (*see above and below*).

George Angell & John Charles Angell John Charles Angell went into business with his eldest son, George Angell. Marks registered in 1840 and 1844. After father's death in 1850 until 1860, George continued the business under the name George Angell & Co., when further marks were registered. Died in 1884.

Arthur Annesley Registered mark as a largeworker in 1758.

Peter Archambo snr Apprenticed to Jacob Margas. Registered marks in 1721, 1722 and 1739. Renowned for prolific output of all standard types of silver ware.

Peter Archambo jnr & Peter Meure Peter Archambo jnr was a cousin of Peter Meure. Mark registered in 1750; usually found on dinner plates.

Hugh Arnett & Edward Pocock Arnett was apprenticed to Isaac Davenport. Arnett & Pocock registered mark in 1720.

William Atkinson Apprenticed to William Bellasis of the Merchant Taylors' Company in 1718 and became a freeman in 1725. Registered two marks in 1725 as a largeworker from the Golden Cup, New Fish Street Hill.

William Bagnall The son of a shop-keeper, apprenticed to Gabriel Sleath in 1736. Registered mark as a largeworker in 1744 from Smithfield.

Thomas Bamford Apprenticed to Charles Adam in 1703. Entered first two marks as a largeworker in 1720 and another in 1739 from Foster Lane. Known as a caster maker as was his master and his apprentice, Samuel Wood.

John Barbe Registered marks as largeworker in 1735, 1739 and 1742.

Edward, John & William Barnard
One of the oldest surviving firms. William served apprenticeship under his father, Edward in 1815. They entered a mark together with William's brother, John in 1829. Known as Edward Barnard & Sons from 1829-1910, and Barnard & Sons Ltd from 1910 to the present day (*see below*).

Edward Barnard, Edward Barnard jnr, John Barnard & William Barnard
Registered their mark together in 1829, as plateworkers (*see above*).

Edward Barnett Apprenticed to Antony Nelme. Registered mark as a largeworker in 1715.

George Baskerville Apprenticed to Joseph Sanders in *c.*1732. Registered marks in 1738, 1745, 1751, 1755 (in partnership with William Sampel) and 1780 (*see below*).

George Baskerville & William Sampel Registered mark together in 1755 (*see above*).

James Le Bass Early 19th-century Dublin maker of ecclesiastical and table silver.

Peter & Jonathan Bateman Peter and Jonathan were sons of Hester Bateman (*see p107*). They entered a mark in 1790 and a further six marks in 1790 (*see below*).

Peter & Ann Bateman Ann married Jonathan Bateman in 1769 and on his death joined in partnership with brother-in-law Peter Bateman, registering a mark with him in 1791 (*see above and below*).

Peter, Ann & William Bateman Ann registered mark with brother-in-law Peter and son William in 1800 (*see above and below*).

Peter & William Bateman Son and grandson of Hester Bateman, registered mark in 1805 (*see above and below*).

William Bateman Born 1774, second son of Jonathan and Ann Bateman, grandson of Hester. Registered marks in partnership with Peter and Ann Bateman in 1800, with Peter only in 1805, and alone in 1815.

In c.1840 sold the family silversmith business to Benjamin Car.

Samuel Bates Marks registered in 1728 and 1744. Liveried in 1752.

Richard Bayley Apprenticed to Charles Overing in 1699, and to John Gibbons in 1704. Became a freeman in 1706. Registered marks in 1708 (from Foster Lane), 1720 and 1739. He was liveried in 1712. His son Richard Bayley was apprenticed to Samuel Spindler. Best-known for his simple domestic wares.

Richard Beale London largeworker. Apprenticed to Jonathan Newton in 1722 and John le Sage in 1725. Three marks are recorded, in 1733, 1739 and 1746.

George Beale London plateworker whose first recorded mark dates from 1699 and second from 1713.

Joseph Bell Apprenticed to Robert Timbrel, later worked in partnership with him. Recorded mark dates from 1716.

William Bell Apprenticed to William Burton in 1748. Marks registered in 1759, 1763, 1769, 1772, 1774 and 1777.

Edward Bennett Apprenticed to Henry Miller in 1720 and Samuel Hutton in 1725. Marks recorded in 1727, 1731, 1737, 1739 and 1747. Liveried in 1737.

John Berthellot Marks registered in 1738, 1739, 1746 and 1750.

John Bettridge Mid-19th century Birmingham silversmith, best known for snuff boxes and other small wares.

Jonathan Bignell Largeworker. Registered marks in 1718 and 1720.

Samuel Blackborrow Apprenticed to William Fawdery. Marks recorded in 1719 and 1721.

Cornelius Bland Served apprenticeship under James Bishop, entered marks in 1772 and 1788. Thomas Young served as his apprentice in 1779 (*see p118*).

James & Elizabeth Bland Elizabeth was the widow of Cornelius. Registered mark in partnership with son James in 1794 (*see previous page*).

William Bond & John Phipps Largeworkers. A mark was recorded in 1754.

Thomas Bolton Prominent early 18th-century Dublin maker of ecclesiastical silverware.

George Boothby Largeworker. Marks registered in 1720 and 1739. Recorded as working from The Parrot in the Strand, hence the parrot in mark.

Matthew Boulton Important Birmingham-based manufacturer. Formed partnership with John Fothergill in 1762-82. Boulton was active in establishing the Birmingham Assay Office. Prior to 1773, when the Birmingham office opened, his silver was marked with Chester mark. Boulton died in 1809 but his manufactory continued throughout the 19th century.

Thomas Bradbury & Sons Sheffield plate manufacturers run by Thomas Bradbury and sons, Joseph and Edward, from 1831. Marks registered in 1860, 1906 and 1907.

Bennett Bradshaw & Co. Apprenticed to Paul de Lamerie (*see p110*) in 1721. Marks of 1737 and 1739 record him in partnership with Robert Tyrill.

John Bridge Apprenticed to William Rogers of Bath; became partner to Philip Rundell (*see p144 and p111*) in 1788. By 1797 they were goldsmiths and jewelers to the king. Bridge registered two marks in 1823, one with a crown. Joined Court in 1831; Prime Warden in 1839. Died 1849.

Walter Brind Apprenticed to John Raynes in 1736 and to his brother, Henry Brind, in 1742. Became a freeman in 1743. Marks recorded in 1749, 1751, 1757 and 1781. Liveried in 1758. Four sons apprenticed to him.

Abel Brokesby Apprenticed to Francis Turner in 1717. Mark recorded in 1727.

James Brooker Mark registered in 1734.

Robert Brown Apprenticed to David Tanqueray in 1723. Registered marks in 1736 and 1739.

Thomas Bumfriss & Orlando Jackson Registered marks as largeworkers in 1766.

Thomas Burridge Marks entered in 1706 and 1720.

Alice & George Burrows Alice was probably the widow of George. Entered marks in partnership with son George in 1801, 1804, 1810 and 1818. Died *c.*1819.

Robert Burton Registered mark as a largeworker in 1758.

William Burwash Registered mark in partnership with Richard Sibley in 1805. Other marks registered alone in 1812 and 1813 (*see below*).

William Burwash & Richard Sibley Mark registered in 1805. Produced high-quality wares in Regency style (*see above*).

Abraham Buteux Buteux was Simon Pantin's godson and probably married Pantin's daughter, Elizabeth. Apprenticed to William West. Registered mark in 1721. Best-known for plain cups, hollow wares and salvers (*see below and p139*).

Elizabeth Buteux Daughter of Simon Pantin and widow of Abraham Buteux. Registered mark on husband's death in 1731. Married Benjamin Godfrey and registered second mark as Elizabeth Godfrey (*see p129*).

Francis Butty & Nicholas Dumee. Registered mark in partnershp some time after 1758.

Elias Cachart Prolific maker of spoons and forks. Registered mark in 1742.

William Cafe Brother of John Cafe (*see p108*), apprenticed to him in 1742 and to Simon Jouet in 1746. Cafe was a prolific maker of cast candlesticks. Registered mark in 1757.

James Anthony Calame Registered two marks in 1765. Known for boxes and watch-cases.

William Caldecott Mark as largeworker recorded in 1756.

Isaac Callard A spoonmaker who registered New Standard and Sterling marks as a largeworker in 1726 from King Street, St Giles. Subsequent marks registered in 1739, 1747 and 1750.

Paul Callard Son of Isaac and Marguerite Callard (*see above*), born 1724. Registered marks in 1752 and 1759.

Edward Capper Registered marks as a smallworker in 1792 and 1813.

Carrington & Company The company was first listed as John Carrington in 1873, becoming Carrington & Company *c*.1880. Specialized in wares for the catering trade. The company still survives today. Marks registered from 1895-1907.

John Carter Maker of candlesticks and salvers. Registered two marks in 1776. Known to have bought candlesticks made and marked in Sheffield which he overstruck with his own mark.

Richard Carter, Daniel Smith & Robert Sharp Registered mark in 1778.

Benjamin Cartwright Goldsmith who registered marks in 1732, 1739, 1748 and 1757. Cartwright snr had a son Benjamin jnr who was also a silversmith.

Thomas Causton Largeworker and possibly pawnbroker. Registered mark in 1731.

Henry Chawner Born 1764, only son of Thomas Chawner (*see next page*). Registered marks in 1786, 1787, and (in partnership with John Emes) 1796. Liveried in 1791. Died in 1851.

Mary Chawner Widow of William Chawner (*see next page*). Registered mark as a spoonmaker in 1834 and five further marks in 1835.

Thomas & William Chawner Brothers who worked together from *c.*1759 (*see below*).

Thomas Chawner Apprenticed to Ebenezer Coker. Registered several marks in 1773, 1775 and 1783. Liveried in 1771 (*see above*).

Charles Chesterman Apprenticed to George Greenhill Jones. Registered marks in 1741, 1752 and 1771. Son Charles was apprenticed to him.

Thomas Clark Apprenticed to Richard Gines in 1719. Registered marks in 1726.

Alexander Coates & Edward French Registered mark in 1734.

Ebenezer Coker Maker of candlesticks, trays and salvers. Apprenticed to Joseph Smith in 1728. Registered marks in 1738, 1739, 1745, 1751 and some time after 1758. Also registered a mark in partnership with Thomas Hammond in 1759/60.

William Comyns & Sons William Comyns established William Comyns & Sons Ltd *c.*1859. Registered first mark in 1859. Sons, Charles Harling Comyns and Richard Harling Comyns, joined *c.*1885. William died in 1916 and Charles in 1925. Formed a limited company in 1930. Richard died in 1953 when the firm was bought by Bernard Copping; survives today. All marks registered as William Comyns & Sons. Last mark registered in 1905.

Edward Cooke Smallworker, apprenticed to Charles Jones in 1713. Registered mark in 1735; liveried in 1737; joined Court of Assistants in 1755.

Matthew Cooper Spoonmaker. Registered marks in 1725 and 1726.

John Cotton & Thomas Head Spoon makers. Registered mark in 1809.

Augustine Courtauld Versatile and prolific maker. Apprenticed to Simon Pantin. Registered marks in 1708, 1729 and 1739. Best-known work is the State Salt of the City of London of 1730.

Samuel Courtauld Maker of rococo-style wares. Son of Augustine Courtauld (*see p108*), he was born in 1720. Apprenticed to father in 1734. Registered marks in 1746 and 1751. Married Louisa Perina Ogier (*see below*).

Louisa Perina Courtauld Maker of domestic wares decorated with classical details. Daughter of Peter Ogier of Poitou; married to Samuel Courtauld in 1749; took over the business on his death in 1765. Formed partnership with George Cowles. Unregistered marks date from *c.*1765 and *c.*1768; registered mark dates from 1777. Died 1807 (*see also above and below and p108*).

Louisa & Samuel Courtauld Born 1752, Samuel was son of Louisa and Samuel Courtauld. Mother and son partnership registered mark in 1777. In 1780 their business was taken over by John Henderson. Samuel died in America in 1821 (*see also p108 and above*).

Louisa Courtauld & George Cowles George Cowles was apprenticed to Louisa's husband, Samuel and to Louisa (*see above*). Registered a mark in partnership *c.*1768. Cowles registered a separate mark in 1777. Died in 1811.

Henry Cowper Registered two marks as a plateworker in 1782.

Robert Albin Cox Maker of general domestic wares including snuff boxes and tea caddies. Apprenticed to Humphrey Payne in 1745 and to John Payne in 1750. Became a freeman in 1752. Registered marks in 1752, 1758 and 1759. Liveried in 1791; elected to Court 1813.

Joseph Cradock & William Reid Registered mark in partnership in 1812, 1819 and 1824.

Ann Craig & John Neville Makers of rococo-style wares. Recorded marks in 1740 and 1742.

Sebastian & James Crespell Huguenot makers, Sebastian and James were probably brothers who may have served apprenticeships with Edward Wakelin. Names appear as suppliers of Wakelin's firm in 1769. Four sons were apprenticed to the trade – André, Sebastian, Honoré and James.

Paul Crespin Much acclaimed Huguenot silversmith. Crespin was apprenticed to Jean Pons. First marks date from *c.*1720. Registered many further marks in 1739, 1740 and 1757. Among his most refined and accomplished pieces are a centrepiece in the Royal Collection and a tureen made for the Duke of Somerset in 1741.

Fenton Creswick & Co. Sheffield-based manufacturers specializing in Sheffield plate, candlesticks and other domestic wares. As T., J. & N. Creswick, registered first mark in 1810. Business was founded by Thomas and James, and Nathaniel joined in 1819. In 1855 the firm became Creswick & Company.

Mark Cripps Son of William Cripps (*see below*). Registered marks in 1767.

William Cripps Prolific silversmith who enjoyed considerable success with his rococo-style wares. Apprenticed to David Willaume jnr in 1731; became a freeman in 1738. Registered marks in 1743, 1746 and 1751. Liveried in 1750.

Richard Crossley & George Smith Spoonmakers who registered mark together in 1807.

John Crouch jnr Son of goldsmith, John Crouch snr, to whom he was apprenticed. Registered mark as partner with Thomas Hannam in 1799 and alone in 1808. Liveried in 1829; died in 1837.

Robert Cruickshank Plateworker. Apprenticed to Alexander Johnston in 1759.

Francis Crump London plateworker. Apprenticed to Gabriel Sleath in 1726; became a freeman in 1741. Registered marks in 1741, 1745, 1751, 1753 (in partnership with Gabriel Sleath) and 1756.

Isaac Dalton Apprenticed to Isaac Davenport in 1711 (*see p124*). Registered two marks in 1711.

Thomas & Jabez Daniell Father and son partnership which dated from c.1771. Thomas entered a mark on his own in 1774.

Thomas Daniell & John Wall Registered mark in 1781. Partnership had dissolved by 1782 when Daniell entered a separate mark (*see also above*).

William Darker Apprenticed to Richard Bailey. Registered marks in 1719, 1720, 1724 and 1731. Liveried in 1725.

Burrage Davenport Active c.1776. No recorded marks. Grimwade identifies mark from a mustard pot.

Isaac Davenport London spoonmaker. Entered mark in 1697, from Gutter Lane. Two further marks registered, one as a largeworker and one as a smallworker c.1697 from Foster Lane.

Samuel Davenport Registered marks in 1786 and, in partnership with Edward Davenport, in 1794. Had a son of the same name who was apprenticed to William Seaman in 1809.

Louis Delisle Registered mark dates from 1775.

John Delmestre Largeworker, registered mark in 1755.

Abraham de Oliveyra Smallworker, largeworker and engraver who may have trained as a goldsmith and engraver in Holland. Registered marks c.1725 and 1739.

Thomas Devonshire & William Watkins Spoonmakers, registered two marks in 1756, and one in 1766.

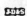

James Dixon & Sons Sheffield-based silversmiths, platers and Britannia metal workers. Started c.1806 by James Willis Dixon; registered marks in 1912 and 1914. James registered marks alone in 1873 and 1910.

J. W. Dobson Henry Holmes Dobson and John Wilkinson Dobson founded the business, which became Dobson & Sons, when Henry was joined by his two sons

Thomas William and Henry Holmes jnr.
Firm specialized in making jewelry and
silverwares, including the Guernsey Race
Cups in 1851. Thomas William and Henry
Holmes registered mark in 1877. Thomas
William registered marks in his own name
for the firm in 1886, 1895 and 1898.

Jane Dorrell & Richard May Jane
Dorrell was the widow of William (also a
silversmith). She registered marks with
Richard May (her apprentice) in 1766, 1769
and 1771.

Louis Dupont Huguenot silversmith and
son of Pierre du Pont, a goldsmith from
Poitiers. Registered marks in 1736 (from
Wardour Street, Soho) and 1739 (from
Compton Street).

John East Apprenticed to George
Garthorne. Registered marks in 1697 and
1721. Liveried in 1708.

Elizabeth Eaton Inherited a prolific firm
of silver spoon and fork manufacturers
*c.*1845 on death of husband, William (*see
below*). In 1858 her son John joined the
firm, which became known as Elizabeth
Eaton & Son. Marks registered in 1845,
1847, 1864 and 1858.

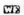

William Eaton Specialized in spoons.
Marks date from 1813, 1824, 1828, 1830,
1834, 1836, 1837 and 1840.

James Charles Edington Registered
marks date from 1828, 1837, 1845, 1854
and 1856.

Edward Edwards Son of John Edwards,
silversmith (*see below*). Apprenticed to John
Mewburn. Registered mark in partnership
with father in 1811, and two alone in 1816.
Edward Edwards' son had same name and
registered marks in 1828, 1840 and 1841.

John Edwards Apprenticed to Thomas
Prichard. Registered marks in partnership
with George Pitches in 1723. Further marks
registered in 1724, 1739 and 1753. Edwards
became Subordinate Goldsmith to the King.

William Edwards Registered marks in
1774 and 1778.

William Edwards Son of Edward Edwards (*see p125*). Apprenticed to his father as an engraver. Registered marks in 1800, 1809 and 1823. Liveried in 1846 and died in 1860.

 John Edwards & George Pitches Registered two marks in partnership in 1723.

 Daniel Egan Early 19th-century Dublin maker of good quality tablewares.

 William Eley snr Apprenticed to William Fearn. Registered mark in partnership with George Pierrepont in 1777. Other marks registered alone in 1778, 1790 and 1795; registered marks in 1797 and 1802 in partnership with William Fearn; and in 1808 with William Chawner and Fearn; final mark without Chawner registered 1814. Eley was liveried in 1806 and died 1824 (*see below*).

 William Eley jnr & William Fearn William Eley jnr was son of William Eley snr (*see above*) and was apprenticed to his father. Registered marks with William Fearn in 1824 (two), 1825 and 1826.

 William Elliott Apprenticed to Richard Gardner. Registered mark in partnership with J.W. Storey in 1809 and alone in 1813.

 John Emes Maker of domestic silverwares, especially tea and coffee services. Apprenticed to William Woollett. Registered mark in partnership with Henry Chawner in 1796 and further marks alone in 1798 and 1802. Business taken over by his wife Rebecca and brother William (*see below*).

 Rebecca Emes & Edward Barnard Important Regency silversmiths, supplied wares to Rundell Bridge & Rundell (*see p111*). Rebecca was the widow of John Emes (*see above*). After partnership with William Emes she registered marks with Edward Barnard (*see p116*) in 1808, 1818, 1821 and 1825.

 Thomas England Goldsmith; apprenticed to John Martin Stocker in 1714 and to Samuel Margas in 1716. Became a freeman in 1728. Two marks, one Sterling and one New Standard, date from 1725. Other marks registered in 1816, 1820 and 1823.

Thomas Eustace Prominent West Country silversmith, apprenticed to Richard Jenkins. Registered mark in 1779. Member of the Exeter Goldsmiths' Company in 1774 and Warden between 1777-1779.

William Fawdery Registered marks date from c.1697 and 1720. Liveried in 1708.

Edward Feline Apprenticed to Augustine Courtauld in 1709. Registered marks in 1720 and 1739. Liveried in 1731.

Fenton Brothers Ltd Specialist cutlers and sword makers from Sheffield. Business was established by John Frederick Fenton and Frank Fenton c.1875. Frank, Samuel and Alfred John Fenton registered marks separately between 1883 and 1888. Firm became Fenton Brothers Ltd in 1896. Supplied ships, hotels and restaurants with their wares.

Edward Fernell Apprenticed to William Grundy in 1762. A mark registered in partnership with Grundy dates from 1779. Subsequent marks were registered alone in 1780, 1781 and (five) in 1787.

Bernard Fletcher Apprenticed to Samuel Lea in 1716. Registered mark in 1725.

Andrew Fogelberg & Stephen Gilbert Registered mark in partnership in 1780. Stephen Gilbert apprenticed to Edward Wakelin and worked in the Wakelin establishment.

John Fossey Son of draper. Apprenticed to Thomas Tearle in 1724; became a freeman in 1731. Marks date from 1733, 1734 and 1739.

Thomas Foster Smallworker. Marks date from 1769 and 1773.

John Fountain Brother of William Fountain (*see p128*). Apprenticed to Robert Grace Cleets and Daniel Smith. Registered marks in 1792, 1793 (in partnership with John Beadnell), and alone in 1797.

William Fountain Younger brother of John (*see p127*). Registered mark in partnership with Pontifex in 1791 and made good-quality silver-gilt baskets. Partnership dissolved by 1794 when William Fountain entered a mark alone.

Charles Fox jnr Maker of a wide variety of high-quality silverware. Son of Charles Fox snr. Entered marks in 1822, 1823 and 1838. Different marks used for various types of ware; the number of marks registered reflect the popularity of Fox's products. Regarded as one of the last craftsmen silversmiths before the mechanization of the mid-19th century.

George Fox Noted English silversmith, probably the son of George Fox of Rundell, Bridge & Rundell. Partner with Charles Fox jnr (*see above*) from *c*.1838 when the latter inherited his father's silver works. Renowned for innovative designs.

Charles Thomas Fox & George Fox Prolific manufacturing silversmiths working in retrospective styles, established in 1801 by James Turner and Charles Fox snr. Charles Fox snr's son (*above*) entered marks in 1841 and 1843.

Thomas Freeman & John Marshall Registered a mark as smallworkers in 1764.

William Frisbee Registered mark with John Edwards (*see p126*) in 1791; another mark of 1792 was recorded alone. Registered mark in partnership with Paul Storr in 1792 (*see p112*).

John Frost Smallworker and largeworker. Apprenticed to Gawen Nash in 1750 and to Thomas Gladwin in 1757. Two marks date from 1757.

Crispin Fuller Registered marks date from 1792, 1796 and 1823. Son Jeremiah apprenticed to James Shallis in 1813.

William Gamble Largeworker. Apprenticed to John Sutton in 1680; became a freeman in 1688. Mark recorded in 1697.

Phillip Garden Goldsmith and jeweler working in the rococo style; apprenticed to

Gawen Nash in 1730. Registered marks in 1738, 1739, 1744, 1748 and 1751. Liveried in 1746; resigned in 1763.

William Garrard Largeworker who was apprenticed to Samuel Laundry in 1729, to Jeffrey Griffith in 1732 and to Ralph Maiden. Registered marks date from 1735, 1739 and 1749.

George Giles Smallworker. Registered mark in 1762; recorded in partnership with John Cooper in 1765.

George Gillingham Apprenticed to Anthony Nelme in 1692. Marks recorded in 1703, 1718 and 1721.

Thomas Gilpin Smallworker and large-worker working in the rococo style. Among his best-known works are candlesticks and tureens in the Althorp collection. Served apprenticeship with John Wells in 1720. Registered marks in 1730 and 1739.

Thomas Gladwin Largeworker; marks date from 1719 and 1737. Daniel Smith became his apprentice in 1740.

Samuel Godbehere Plateworker. Registered marks in 1784 (two), 1786 (in partnership with Edward Wigan); 1789, 1792, 1800 (in partnership with Edward Wigan and James Bult, as Samuel Godbehere & Company); and in 1818 (in partnership with James Bult). Godbehere probably had connections with the city of Bath, as he was given power of attorney for the signing of the entry into the register of two Bath goldsmiths, William Bottle and James Burden.

Philip Goddard Largeworker and small-worker who was apprenticed to Peter White in 1711. Became a freeman in 1720. Registered marks in 1725 and 1738 from Fountain Court, Cheapside.

Benjamin Godfrey Largeworker. Married Elizabeth Buteux (*see p119*) in 1732. Registered marks in 1732 and 1739.

Benjamin Godwin Largeworker. Apprenticed to Joseph Clare in 1722 and William Darker in 1727. Registered a mark in 1730.

Richard Gosling Smallworker. Apprenticed to Matthew Cuthbert in 1712. Registered marks in 1733, 1739 and 1748. Goldsmith Company convicted him of counterfeiting marks but the business was continued by sons Richard and Joseph.

James Gould Candlestick maker, brother of William Gould. Apprenticed to David Green in 1714. Marks recorded in 1722 (one New Standard and one Sterling), c.1733, 1739 and 1743.

William Gould Candlestick maker, whose most famous work is the Knesworth chandelier made for the Fishmongers' Company in 1752. Apprenticed to his brother James Gould in 1724. Registered marks in 1732, 1734, 1739, 1748 and 1753.

Henry Greene Largeworker apprenticed to Thomas Allen in 1693. Registered marks in 1700 and 1720. Liveried in 1708.

Samuel Green Apprenticed to Richard Gines in 1714. Became a freeman in 1721. Three marks recorded in 1721, two Sterling and one New Standard.

William Grundy Largeworker, apprenticed to Edward Vincent in 1731. Registered marks in 1743, 1748, 1777, and in 1779 in partnership with Edward Fernell (*see below*).

William Grundy & Edward Fernell Fernell was apprenticed to Grundy in 1762. They registered mark in partnership in 1779. Fernell registered a mark on his own in 1780, possibly after Grundy's death (*see above*).

Thomas & James Guest & Joseph Cradock Father and son entered marks in partnership with Joseph Cradock in 1806 and 1808.

Louis Guichard Largeworker, possibly of Huguenot descent. Recorded a mark in 1748.

Nathaniel Gulliver Apprenticed to Jonathan Newton in 1715, and to Ambrose Stevenson in 1716. Registered mark in 1722.

Richard Gurney & Co. Largeworker, apprenticed to Richard Bayley in 1717. Became a freeman in 1724. Registered his first mark in partnership with Thomas Cook in 1727. Trading as Richard Gurney & Co. the company registered marks in 1734, 1739, 1749 and 1750. Richard's younger brother John was apprenticed to him in 1730.

William Gwillim & Peter Castle Gwillim was apprenticed to John Gamon in 1731. Peter Castle was apprenticed to Thomas Ruch in 1734 and became a freeman c.1741. They registered a mark in partnership in 1744.

Martin Hall & Co. of Sheffield Prominent Sheffield manufacturer founded in 1854 by Ebenezer Hall and Robert Martin. Made a wide variety of good-quality tablewares.

William Hall Apprenticed to Jonathan Bateman in 1787 and to Ann Bateman in 1791. Registered mark in 1795.

Henry Hallsworth Prolific producer of candlesticks. Apprenticed to William Cafe in 1762 (*see p119*). Recorded mark c.1769.

John Hamilton Prominent Dublin maker of early 18th century. Made variety of tablewares including cutlery and plates.

Lewis Hamon Maker of rare rococo-style wares. Registered marks in 1736, 1738 and 1739.

Messrs Hancock & Co. Engraver and silversmith Charles Frederick Hancock worked with Storr and Mortimer until 1843 when he founded his own business. He made presentation pieces and silver sculpture. Hancock & Co. is still in business as a retailer.

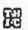

Thomas Hannam & John Crouch Salver, tray and candlestick makers active c.1773. Thomas Hannam had previously formed partnership with Richard Mills with whom he registered a mark in 1765.

Joseph Hardy & Thomas Lowndes Registered mark in partnership in 1798.

Harrison Bros. & Howson Sheffield-based manufacturers of domestic wares, cutlery and electroplate, run by James William Harrison, Henry Harrison and William Howson. The business began in 1866. Marks were registered by the partners separately: George in 1896, Henry in 1880 and William in 1866.

John Harvey Largeworker. Served apprenticeship under Matthew Judkins; became a freeman in 1737. Registered marks date from 1738, 1739 (two), 1745, 1746, 1748 and 1750.

Samuel Harwood Sheffield manufacturer of spoons and cutlery. Registered marks in 1835 and 1836.

Charles Hatfield Silversmith who made high-quality pieces which reflect Huguenot designs. Served apprenticeship under Joseph Barbutt and David Williams. Registered marks in 1727 and 1739. Died *c.*1740 when his mother or widow Susannah Hatfield registered a mark.

Hawksworth, Eyre & Co. Sheffield- and London-based manufacturers of silver and plate. Charles Hawksworth and John Eyre set up the firm in 1852. Marks registered in 1862, 1900 and 1912.

Thomas & George Hayter Thomas, together with son George, registered mark in 1816.

Thomas Heming Maker of high-quality silverware. Served apprenticeship under Peter Archambo (*see p119*). Registered marks in 1745 and *c.*1767. Appointed Principal Goldsmith to the King in 1760 and from this date a crown appeared above his mark until 1782, when he was replaced by Jeffreys & Jones. Liveried in 1763. Earlier pieces are often highly elegant reflecting the influence of Archambo.

George Heming & William Chawner Registered marks in partnership in 1774 and 1781.

David Hennell Largeworker. Apprenticed to Edward Wood in 1728. Registered marks in 1736, 1763 (in partnership with his son)

and 1768. Son Robert was apprenticed to him in 1756. Liveried in 1763 and retired from business in 1773 *(see below)*.

Robert Hennell Maker of good-quality small domestic silverwares such as baskets, salt cellars and epergnes. Born in 1741, son of David Hennell to whom he was apprenticed in 1756. Registered marks in partnership with father in 1763 and 1768, and alone in 1772 and 1773. By 1795, registered mark in partnership with son David; mark of 1802 was registered with David and a second son, Samuel. Worked until death in 1811, when his son Samuel took over with the registration of his own mark in 1812 *(see also p110)*.

David and Robert Hennell Registered mark together in 1763. Marks usually found on fine small silver ware *(see above, below and p110)*.

Robert, David & Samuel Hennell David was the son of Robert and brother of Samuel. Apprenticed to father in 1782. Father and sons registered two marks in 1802 *(see also above below and p110)*.

Robert and Samuel Hennell Samuel was Robert's son, and registered a mark in partnership with father and his brother David in 1802; mark registered by Samuel and Robert only in 1802 *(see also above below and p110)*.

Henry Herbert Largeworker, possibly of Huguenot origins. Became subordinate Goldsmith to the King from 1736-1740. Registered marks in 1734, 1735, 1739 and 1748.

Samuel Herbert Largeworker, maker of pierced baskets and epergnes of Foster Lane. Registered marks in 1747 and, with an unnamed partner, as Samuel Herbert & Co. in 1750.

Lewis Herne & Francis Butty Registered a mark in partnership as largeworkers in 1757.

Ann Hill Registered mark in 1726, from Great Trinity Lane, and a second mark c.1735.

George Hindmarsh Registered mark in partnership with Robert Abercromby in 1731 (see p114) and alone in 1731, c.1736, 1739 and 1753.

 Samuel Hitchcock Largeworker, apprenticed to John Brace in 1699. Registered marks in 1713, 1720 and 1730. Liveried in 1721 and resigned in 1743.

 Sarah Holaday Largeworker. Registered mark in 1719 and (Sterling) 1725.

 William Holmes & Nicholas Dumée Registered mark in partnership in 1773. Holmes registered marks alone in 1776 and 1792. J. S. Denwall and his son John Gwyn Holmes served as his apprentices.

 John Hopkins Served as an apprentice under Andrew Archer in 1716 and became a freeman in 1723. Registered two marks, one Sterling and one New Standard, both undated c.1720-4.

 Charles Hougham Plate and buckle-maker, apprenticed to Henry Corry in 1764. Registered marks in 1769, 1773, 1779, 1785 and seven more marks in 1786.

 Solomon Howland Apprenticed to Thomas Whipham in 1752 and to Edward Day in 1759. Became a freeman in 1760. Registered two marks in 1760.

 John S. Hunt Plateworker. A partner in Mortimer & Hunt from 1839-1844. Company became Hunt & Roskill when Mortimer retired in 1843. Hunt registered marks in 1839, 1844 and 1855. Marks were registered as Hunt & Roskill Ltd in 1897, 1901 and 1912.

 Samuel Hutton Largeworker. Apprenticed to Edward Jennings in 1717; became a freeman in 1724. Marks recorded in 1724, 1725, 1734 and 1740.

 John Hyatt & Charles Semore Registered mark in partnership in 1757.

 John Jacobs Largeworker, possibly of Huguenot origin, made baskets, candlesticks and domestic items in rococo style. Registered marks in 1734 and 1739.

Edward Jay Largeworker, apprenticed to Gabriel Sleath in 1743. Registered mark in 1757.

Charles Frederick Kandler Important maker of the mid-18th century, possibly of German descent. Registered marks as a largeworker in partnership with James Murray in 1727 from Saint Martin's Lane; further marks registered on his own, one undated and others in 1739 and 1768.

James Keating Late 18th-century Dublin maker, renowned for boxes.

David King Early 18th-century Dublin maker of good-quality ecclesiastic and domestic silverware.

Jeremiah King Apprenticed to William Scarlett, became a freeman in 1722. Registered New Standard and Sterling marks in 1723; other marks recorded 1736, 1739, 1743 and 1744.

William King Registered marks in 1820, 1826 and 1829.

Henry Lake John Elliott Lake & Son was established in 1833 by Henry Lake in Exeter. From 1874 the firm continued under direction of son John Elliot, who was joined by his son John Henry. John Elliott Lake and John Henry Lake registered a mark in 1903.

George Lambe Largeworker and maker of flatware, apprenticed to Joseph Barbutt in 1706. Registered a mark in 1713.

Jane Lambe Largeworker. Widow of George Lambe (*see above*). Registered two undated marks *c.*1719-1722.

Edward Lambe Largeworker. Son of George Lambe. Apprenticed to mother Jane Lambe in 1731. Registered marks in 1740 and 1742. Lambe had two sons John and George who were also silversmiths (*see below*).

John Lambe Spoonmaker and watch-maker. Son of Edward Lambe (*see above*). Marks recorded in 1774, 1780, 1782, 1783, 1785, 1788, 1790 and 1791.

John Lampfert Spoonmaker and large-worker. Registered marks in 1748 and 1749.

John Langford & John Sebille Plate-workers. Mark attributed to them found by Chaffers on an inkstand of 1763 seems certain to be theirs because of the combination of their initials. Mark appears mainly on pierced baskets.

James Langlois Huguenot silversmith. Registered mark in 1738.

Louis Laroche French maker. Registered marks in 1725 and 1739. He was found guilty of counterfeiting marks by the Goldsmiths' Company.

John Laughlin Mid-18th-century Dublin maker of a variety of unusually designed tablewares.

Samuel Laundy Largeworker possibly of Huguenot origin. Apprenticed to James Goodwin in 1720. Registered marks in 1727, 1731 (in partnership with Jeffrey Griffith) and alone in 1732.

Thomas & Daniel Leader Prominent Sheffield-based silver manufacturers of the early 19th century.

Abraham Le Francis Soho-based large-worker. Registered marks *c.*1742 and in 1746 from West Street, Seven Dials.

Augustin Le Sage Jeweler, son of John Hugh Le Sage and younger brother of Simon (*see below*). Mark possibly registered in the middle of the 18th century. A tureen of 1774 bearing his mark carries the golden cup which is also on his father's and brother's marks.

John Hugh Le Sage Huguenot silversmith, father of Augustin and Simon (*see above and below*). Apprenticed to Lewis Curey in 1708. Registered marks in 1718, 1722 and 1739. Liveried in 1740; became Subordinate Goldsmith to the King.

Simon Le Sage Son of goldsmith John Hugh Le Sage (*see above*). Apprenticed to father in 1742 and later to Peter Meure. Registered marks in 1754. Subordinate

Goldsmith to the King from c.1754-1759 and produced many Royal commisssions.

Charles Leslie One of the most highly-regarded Dublin makers of the mid-18th century. Mark recorded on cake baskets and table wares.

John & Henry Lias Father and son registered marks as spoonmakers in 1818 and 1819.

John, Henry & Charles Lias Charles was junior partner to father John and brother Henry. Registered a mark together in 1823.

John Lingard Largeworker; apprenticed to William Fawdery in 1709. Registered marks in 1718, 1719 and 1720.

Seth Lofthouse Largeworker, apprenticed to William Wakefield in 1676. Recorded mark dates from c.1699. Active until c.1722.

Matthew Lofthouse Apprenticed to George Hanson of the Wax Chandlers' Company in 1689 and made free in 1697. Registered marks in 1705 and 1721.

Mary Lofthouse Largeworker. Widow of Matthew or Seth Lofthouse. Registered marks in 1731.

William Looker Largeworker; apprenticed to Benjamin Bentley in 1706; became a freeman in 1713. Registered marks in 1713 and 1720.

Edward Lowe Smallworker and plate-worker. Registered marks in 1760, 1769, 1770, 1771 and 1777.

Robert Lucas Largeworker. Registered marks in 1727 and 1739 from Lombard Street and Bow Lane.

John Ludlow Largeworker; apprenticed to George Cox in 1706; became a freeman in 1713. Registered marks in 1713 and 1720.

Jonathan Madden Registered only known mark in 1702 from Ball Alley, Lombard Street.

James Maitland Apprenticed to John Pero in 1718. Registered mark without date c.1728.

 Robert Makepeace & Richard Carter Registered mark together in 1777. In 1778, Richard Carter recorded a new mark as a plateworker.

 Thomas Mann Largeworker; apprenticed to William Juson in 1706 and to Henry Clark. Registered marks in 1713, 1720, 1729, 1736 and 1739.

 James Manners Registered marks in 1726, 1734 and 1739. His son James Manners jnr was also a silversmith, registering a mark in 1744.

 Mappin & Webb Prominent English engravers, silversmiths and cutlers, still thriving today. Company founded by Joseph Mappin in Sheffield in 1810. Taken over by sons as Mappin Brothers, who later joined with a brother-in-law to become Mappin & Webb. Began producing good-quality electroplate silverware in the mid-19th century; now concerned mainly with jewelry. Earlier marks were registered by John Newton Webb and George Webb, plateworkers, in 1866 and 1880. As Mappin & Webb Limited they registered marks in 1899 and 1900.

 Thomas Mercer Largeworker, apprenticed to William Gardiner in 1722 and to Aaron Bates in 1728. Registered only mark in 1740.

 George Methuen Largeworker, who produced good quality salvers and dishes. Registered mark in 1743.

 Nathanial Mills Prolific Birmingham-based manufacturer of snuff boxes, vinaigrettes, wine labels and other small wares.

 James Mince & William Hodgkins Plateworkers, registered mark in 1780.

 Thomas Moore Largeworker of mid-18th century; apprenticed to George Greenhill Jones in 1743. Registered mark in 1750.

James Morison Largeworker. Registered mark in 1740. Son Richard was apprenticed to him in 1776, as was William Holinshed in 1780.

John Motherby Plateworker, apprenticed to Joseph Barbett. Registered mark in 1719.

J. R. Neill Important mid-19th-century Dublin retailer of good-quality silverware.

Anthony Nelme Prominent manufacturer of civic regalia, especially maces and toilet services. His work often reflects the influence of Huguenot design. Mark registered in 1697. Elected Assistant to the Court of Goldsmiths in 1703 and made Warden in 1717 and 1722.

Francis Nelme Son of Anthony Nelme (*see above*) and apprenticed to him in 1712. Marks registered in 1723 and 1739. He was not as successful as his father.

Hannah Northcote Born in 1761, the daughter of Simeon Coley, bucklemaker, and wife of Thomas Northcote (*see below*). Registered first mark after husband's death in 1798 and another in 1799. Died in 1831.

Thomas Northcote Plateworker and spoonmaker. Registered marks in 1776, 1777, 1779, 1782, 1784 (two), and a further four between then and 1794, when he registered a mark in partnership with George Bourne.

Henry Nutting Plateworker; apprenticed to Charles Wright in 1782 and Thomas Chawner in 1784. Registered mark in 1796. Later mark registered with Robert Hennell (*see p133*).

Isaac D'Olier Mid-18th-century Dublin maker of good-quality spoons, sauceboats and tablewares.

Francis Pages Maker of standard domestic wares; apprenticed to David Williams in 1718. Registered marks in 1729 and 1739. Liveried 1737.

Simon Pantin Huguenot maker of the early 18th century. Produced considerable quantities of plate. Daughter married Peter

Courtauld. Registered marks as a large-worker in 1701; his son Simon jnr was also a silversmith.

 Richard Pargeter Apprenticed to Andrew Archer in 1718 and to James Wilkes in 1724; became a freeman in 1726. Registered marks in 1730, 1737 and 1739. Pargeter was illiterate and signed his name with an "X". Liveried in 1737.

John Parker & Edward Wakelin Largeworkers. Mark registered *c.*1758. Although Wakelin was in the business first, it is Parker's initials which appear above in their mark – probably indicating seniority in finance rather than skill. The partnership seems to have continued until 1776 when Wakelin took William Taylor as his partner.

Thomas Parr Son of Thomas Parr (also a silversmith). Registered marks in 1733 and 1739. Liveried in 1750; joined Court in 1735 and was a Warden from 1771 to 1773.

 A. & F. Parsons (of Edward Tessier) Arthur Martin Parsons and Frank Herbert Parsons continued the business of Edward Tessier (or Vander & Hedges, as it was also called). Registered marks in 1910 and 1911. The company became Tessiers Ltd in 1920, with the Parsons as first directors. It continues today as one of London's most well-established dealers.

 Humphrey Payne Largeworker who produced plain domestic wares, particularly cups and tankards. Apprenticed to Roger Grange in 1694; became a freeman in 1701. Registered marks in 1701, 1720 and 1739. Liveried in 1708; became a member of Court in 1734 and was made a Warden from 1747-9.

 John Payne Son of Humphrey Payne (*see above*); apprenticed to him in 1733. Registered mark in 1751. Liveried in 1740.

 Thomas & Richard Payne Plateworkers; sons of John Payne (*see above*). Registered their mark in partnership in 1777.

 Edmund Pearce Apprenticed to Henry Beesley in 1693 and to Phillip Rollos in 1697. Registered marks in 1705 and 1720.

Richard Pearce & George Burrows
Plateworkers. Registered marks together in
1826 and 1835.

Wiliam & Robert Peaston Largeworkers in partnership from 1756 until
1763. Registered mark in 1756.

Abraham Peterson Plateworker. Registered first mark in partnership with Peter
Podio in 1783, and second alone in 1792
(*see p142*).

Phillip Phillis Largeworker. Registered
two marks in 1720. Liveried in 1721.

S. J. Phillips Well-known retail business
of silversmiths and jewelers founded in 1869
by Solomon Joel. Firm continued by son,
Edmund A. Phillips. Mark registered in
1901.

Thomas Phipps & Edward Robinson
Thomas was son of James Phipps and
apprenticed to him in 1769. Phipps &
Robinson entered marks in 1783 and 1789.
They were later joined by James Phipps
(Thomas's son). Final mark of 1816 was
registered by father and son.

Pezé Pilleau The son of Pezé Pilleau snr.
Maker of fine-quality, often highly original
wares. Apprenticed to John Charter in
1710. Registered two marks, undated,
between 1720 and 1724 and a third in 1739.

John Pittar Late 18th-century Dublin
maker of good-quality spoons and other
wares.

William Pitts Plateworker, known for
epergnes, baskets and neo-rococo candlesticks. Son of Thomas Phillip; apprenticed to
him in 1769. Registered marks in 1781,
1786, 1791 and 1806.

William Pitts & Joseph Preedy
William Pitts registered mark in partnership
with Preedy in 1791. Partnership dissolved
by 1799, when Pitts entered mark on his
own (*see also above*).

William Playfair & William Wilson
Spoonmakers; partners in Playfair Wilson
& Co. Registered mark in 1782.

Charles & John Plumley Charles registered mark alone in 1830, and with John Plumley in 1822.

William Plummer Plateworker known for pierced silverwares such as cake baskets and strainers. Apprenticed to Edward Aldridge in *c.*1746; registered marks in 1755, 1774 and 1789.

Peter Podio Plateworker; registered mark in partnership with Abraham Peterson from Primrose Hill in 1783, and alone in 1790 (*see p141*).

Thomas Boulton Pratt & Arthur Humphreys Partners registered mark as plateworkers in 1780. Pratt's son, Thomas, was apprenticed to him in 1785. Two other sons, Tom and James, were also silversmiths and served apprenticeship under him.

Joseph Preedy Plateworker; apprenticed to Thomas Whipham in 1765 and, in 1766, to William Plummer. Registered first marks alone in 1777, second in partnership with William Pitts in 1791 (*see p141*) and third alone in 1800.

John Priest Specialist candlestick maker; apprenticed to William Gould in 1739. Registered mark as largeworker in 1748.

William & James Priest William and James Priest were probably brothers. James Priest was apprenticed to William in 1750. Mark as largeworkers appears from *c.*1764. They are recorded working together until 1773.

Edwin Charles Purdee Plateworker. Registered marks in 1876 (two), 1883 and 1895.

Benjamin Pyne Important maker of civic and ecclesiastical regalia; apprenticed to George Bowers in 1667. Mark registered in 1696, further mark registered undated. He was Subordinate Goldsmith to the King for the Coronation of George I.

John Quantock Specialist candlestick maker of the mid-18th century; apprenticed to James Gould in 1726. Registered marks after 1739 and in 1754.

Philip Rainaud Huguenot maker of rare domestic silverware; apprenticed to Pierre Platel (*see p111*) in 1700. Registered marks in 1708 and 1720. Liveried in 1721.

Abel Ram Dublin maker of late 17th century. Known for the high quality of his workmanship; specialized in making communion plate.

Charles Rawlings & William Summers Plateworker, particularly associated with high-quality snuffboxes. Registered mark in partnership in 1829 and a further six new marks in 1840.

Charles Reily & George Storer Makers of good-quality small wares, especiallly snuff boxes. Registered mark in 1829 and in 1840.

Isaac Ribouleau Maker of rare high-quality wares; apprenticed to Augustine Courtauld in 1716 (*see p121*). Entered two marks *c.*1723.

Richard Richardson Sheffield manufacturer of silver and electroplate domestic wares. Business established in 1796. Registered mark in 1895.

George Ridout Registered his only mark as a largeworker in 1743.

Roberts & Belk Sheffield company established in 1809/10 as Furniss, Pole & Turner. Samuel Roberts and Charles Belk formed partnership in 1885. Samuel retired in 1879 and was succeeded by Charles. The firm became a limited company in 1901 and still exists today. As Samuel Roberts & Charles Belk marks were registered in 1865 and 1878. Marks as Roberts & Belk Ltd were registered in 1906 and 1938.

Thomas Robins Maker who specialized in dinner plates and entrée dishes. Apprenticed to cousin John Robins in 1786. Registered mark in 1801. Liveried in 1811; died in 1859.

John Robinson Apprenticed to Thomas Bayley in 1727. Registered marks in 1738 and 1739.

John Roker Largeworker. Son of Philip Roker (*see below*); apprenticed to him in 1737. Registered mark in 1743.

 Philip Roker Maker of spoons and other wares; apprenticed to Joseph Barbutt, specialist spoonmaker in 1707. Registered marks in 1720 and 1739. Sons Matthew and John and wife Elizabeth were also silversmiths (*see above and below*).

 Matthew Roker Son of Philip and Elizabeth Roker (*see above and below*). Registered first mark as a largeworker in 1755. He continued his father's business.

 Elizabeth Roker Widow of Philip Roker (*see above*). Registered mark as a plateworker in 1776.

 Emick Romer (Emmich Römer) Mid-18th-century Norwegian plateworker working in London from c.1758–1795. Son of an Oslo goldsmith, Romer, born in 1724, lived in Bragernaes prior to coming to London. Registered mark c.1758.

 Etienne Rongent Huguenot jeweler and silversmith. Registered only mark as largeworker c.1731.

 Mary Rood Possibly the widow of James Rood (also a silversmith). Registered two marks as a largeworker in 1721, one Sterling and one New Standard.

 Alexander Roode Apprenticed to John Ruslen in 1669. Registered mark in 1697. Liveried in 1687.

 Gundry Roode Largeworker of the early 18th century; apprenticed to Alexander Roode (*see above*). Registered marks in 1710, 1721 and 1737.

 Richard Rugg Largeworker; apprenticed to James Gould (*see p130*) in 1738. Registered marks in 1754 and 1775. Son Richard was apprenticed to him in 1763. Liveried in 1772; died c.1795–1801. Mark similar to that of Robert Rew.

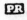 **Philip Rundell** Partner in one of the leading silver manufacturers of the late 18th/early 19th centuries (*see p111*).

Rundell was apprenticed to William Rogers, jeweler, of Bath and arrived in London *c*.1768. Worked for Theed and Pickett, made a partner with Pickett in 1772 and became sole owner between 1785 and 1786. Took John Bridge as partner in 1788 and nephew Edmund Waller Rundell as partner in 1803, by which time the company had become Rundell, Bridge & Rundell. Registered marks in 1819 and 1822. Appointed Goldsmith and Jeweler to the King in 1797. Retired from his business *c*.1823, when John Bridge registered his own mark.

Thomas Sadler Largeworker; apprenticed to Lawrence Cole in 1692. Registered marks in 1701 and *c*.1720. Liveried in 1705.

Joseph Sanders Plateworker; apprenticed to Thomas Eweds in 1714, and Joseph Belcher in 1719. Registered marks in 1730 and 1739. Liveried in 1727/8.

Adey, Joseph & Albert Savory Albert was the son of Adey and brother of Joseph. Registered marks together in 1833 and 1834. Further marks registered by Albert and Joseph only in 1735, as A. B. Savory & Sons.

Richard Scarlett Son of William Scarlett; apprenticed to him in 1710. Registered marks in 1720 and 1723 (*see below*).

William Scarlett Apprenticed to Simon Scott in 1687. Registered marks *c*.1697, 1720, 1722 and 1725.

John Schofield Prominent plateworker, known for candlesticks, candelabra and silver-mounted glass. Registered mark in 1776 in partnership with Robert Jones and further marks alone in 1787 and 1778. He also worked for the retailers and royal goldsmiths Jeffreys, Jones & Gilbert.

William Schofield Spoonmaker; apprenticed to George Grace in 1786. Registered marks in 1820 and 1833.

John Schuppe Probably of Dutch origin, particularly known for cow creamers and other small wares. Registered mark as a largeworker in 1753.

John Scofield Specialized in candlesticks and candelabra. Registered mark as a plateworker in partnership with Robert Jones in 1776 and further marks alone in 1778 and 1787.

 Digby Scott & Benjamin Smith Birmingham-based silversmiths who also worked with Matthew Boulton (*see p118*). Scott and Smith entered a mark in partnership in 1802 and 1803. In 1807 Smith registered a mark alone.

 William Shaw Apprenticed to Edward Holliday in 1715. Registered marks in 1729, 1739 and 1745.

 William Shaw & William Priest Makers of coffee pots, tankards and other domestic hollow wares. Registered mark in 1749.

 Alice Sheene Widow of Joseph Sheene silversmith. Mark registered in 1700.

 Thomas Shermer Apprenticed to Richard Bailey in 1708. Registered mark in 1717.

 James Shruder Maker of rococo-style wares, possibly of German origin. Registered marks in 1737 and 1739.

 Richard Sibley Regency maker of high-quality wares. Son of John Sibley of Bath; apprenticed to Daniel Smith and in 1791 to Robert Sharp. Registered mark in partnership with Thomas Ellerton in 1803, alone in 1805, in partnership with William Burwash in 1805 and alone in 1812. Liveried in 1811. Had various apprentices, including son Richard in 1821.

 William Simons Apprenticed to Richard Hawkins in 1757 and to Robert Salmon, spoonmaker. Registered two marks in 1776. In 1776 George Whittingham was apprenticed to him as a spoonmaker.

 James Slater Apprenticed to John Ford in 1718, and to Thomas Kidder and John Allbright. Registered mark *c.*1725.

 Daniel Sleamaker Apprenticed to Robert Timberley in 1691. Registered marks date from 1701 (in partnership with John Read) and 1704.

Gabriel Sleath Maker of a substantial numbers of medium-quality domestic hollow wares, such as coffee pots, tankards and cups. Apprenticed to Thomas Cooper in 1691. Registered marks in 1707, 1720, 1739 and 1753 (in partnership with Francis Crump, *see below*). Liveried in 1712.

Gabriel Sleath & Francis Crump Sleath and apprentice Francis Crump registered mark in 1753 (*see also above*).

William Robert Smiley Maker of cutlery, plate and wedding rings, and dealer in second-hand plate. Registered marks in 1842 and 1844, and many more as a spoonmaker until final one in 1857.

Daniel Smith & Robert Sharp Makers of high-quality wares in classical style, especially racing cups, candelabra and dinner plates. Registered mark in *c.*1763. Mark registered with a new partner, Richard Carter in 1778, and a further mark without Carter in 1780. May have supplied wares to Parker & Wakelin.

James Smith Apprenticed to Peter White in 1710; became a freeman in 1718. Registered marks in 1720 and 1718.

George Smith Prolific maker of spoons and other flatwares. Registered marks in 1774, 1775, 1776, 1778, 1780, 1782 and (in partnership with William Fearn) 1786.

George Smith & Thomas Hayter Hayter was apprenticed to George Smith in 1782. Registered mark in partnership with Smith's son George in 1792.

Nathanial Smith & Company Prominent Sheffield silversmith. Made candlesticks, casters and other domestic wares.

William Smith snr Apprenticed to his father Samuel Smith in 1742; freedom 1749. Registered marks as a smallworker in 1758, 1763, 1764, 1769 and 1774. A parliamentary report of 1773 records that Smith gave evidence against Sheffield manufacturers from whom he had purchased substandard punch ladles. Died *c.*1781.

William Soame Apprenticed to Samuel Hitchcock in 1713. Registered two marks in 1723; further marks date from 1732 and 1739.

Francis Spilsbury snr Apprenticed to Richard Green in 1708. Registered marks in 1729 and 1739. Liveried in 1737.

Francis Spilsbury jnr Maker of small domestic wares such as cruets and salts. Son of Francis Spilsbury (*see above*). Registered mark in 1767. Liveried in 1763.

Nicholas Sprimont Important Huguenot maker, Sprimont was born in Liège in 1716. Registered first mark in 1743. In 1748 he became a full-time porcelain manufacturer. Died in 1754. Any surviving marked pieces of his are extremely rare and were made between 1742 and 1747.

George Squire Apprenticed to John Brace in 1699. Registered two marks in 1720.

Ambrose Stevenson Apprenticed to father Thomas Stevenson in 1692. Registered marks in 1707 and 1720.

John Stone Spoonmaker based in Exeter. Registered mark in 1844.

J. W. Story & W. Elliott Registered mark as plateworkers in partnership in 1809 (*see also p126*).

William Sumner Apprenticed to Thomas Chawner in 1763. Registered marks in 1775 (in partnership with Richard Crossley), alone in 1776, 1777, 1780, 1782, 1784, and various further marks before his last in 1803. Mary Sumner, his wife, recorded a mark in 1807 when William had probably died (*see also below*).

William Sumner & Richard Crossley Registered mark in 1775 (*see also above*).

William Sutton The brother of James Sutton (also a registered silversmith). Registered two marks in 1784.

John Swift Maker of rococo and chinoiserie-decorated domestic wares. Registered marks *c.*1728, 1739, and two in 1757. Son John apprenticed to him in 1750.

David Tanqueray Prominent maker of lavish rococo-style pieces and domestic wares, including a gilt wine cistern of 1718 at Chatsworth. Registered marks in 1713 and 1720.

Ann Tanqueray Widow of David Tanqueray (*see above*). Registered two marks on the death of her husband *c.*1725. She was probably not a Goldsmith herself as wares bearing her mark were clearly made by journeymen she employed.

William Tant Maker of flatwares. Son of a buckle carver. Mark is undated but was probably recorded *c.*1766.

John Tayler Apprenticed to Henry Green in 1714. Registered marks in 1728 and 1734.

Joseph Hayes Taylor Birmingham-based silversmith who produced small items and jewelry. Registered mark in 1880; went out of business in 1888.

Samuel Taylor Maker specializing in tea-caddies and sugar bowls, often decorated with floral chasing. Apprenticed to John Newton in 1737. Registered marks in 1744 and 1757.

Thomas Tearle Maker of cups and salvers; apprenticed to Gabriel Sleath in 1707. Registered marks in 170, 1720 and 1739 (*see p147*).

William Theobalds & Lockington Bunn Registered mark in 1839.

Thomas & Co. Bond Street Retail silversmiths established by John William Thomas in 1759. Francis Bourne Thomas took control *c.*1871 and the name changed to F. B. Thomas & Co. Francis registered first marks in 1874. In 1900 John William Thomas and C. H. Townly took over and continued the business until *c.*1941 when an air raid demolished it. Further marks were registered in 1875 and 1887.

Elizabeth Tookey The widow of James Tookey and the mother of Thomas. She was a spoonmaker. Her mark would have been entered in part of the register which is now missing and the date is not recorded (*see below*).

James Tookey Maker of flatwares. Registered marks in 1750 and 1762; liveried in 1758. Married Elizabeth Tookey. Son Thomas served as apprentice in 1766 (*see above and below*).

Thomas Tookey Son of James Tookey, spoonmaker, apprenticed to him in 1766. Registered marks in 1773, 1775, 1779 and 1780.

Charles Townsend Dublin maker of quality wares. Mark recorded on Communion cup and two-handled cup.

Tudor & Leader Prominent Sheffield silversmiths. Made domestic hollow-wares such as sauce tureens.

John Tuite Salver-maker; apprenticed to John Matthews of Dublin in 1703. Worked in Dublin between 1710 and 1720, where he used a similar mark to the one he later registered in London. Moved to London in 1723 and registered an undated mark *c.*1724 and another in 1739.

William Tuite Registered mark as a largeworker, undated, but between 1755 and 1758.

Walter Tweedie Late 18th-century spoonmaker and plateworker. Registered marks in 1775, 1779 and 1781.

George Unite Unite & Sons were established in Birmingham in 1825 by George Unite. In 1852 they were listed in London as silversmiths. Registered marks date from 1886 and 1889.

Aymé Videau Important Huguenot silversmith, especially associated with good-quality domestic wares, often decorated with flat chasing. Apprenticed to David Willaume in 1723. Recorded marks date from 1739; an earlier mark is probably missing from the register. Liveried in 1746.

Edward Vincent Maker of good-quality domestic wares, such as coffeee pots, salvers and cups. There is some uncertainty about his identity and he is only identifiable by a mark registered in 1739. Another mark attributed to him dates from *c.*1720.

Edward Wakelin Partner in important firm of silversmiths; apprenticed to John le Sage in 1730. By 1747 he had joined George Wickes and registered first mark in 1747 (very similar to that of Wickes). Wakelin took over the business and appointed a new partner, John Parker, *c.*1758. From 1761 the business became Parker & Wakelin Partnership, with Parker as senior partner. Wakelin continued in business until 1777 when his son John and William Taylor joined the firm. Wakelin's work from 1760 to 1770 reflects the influence of French designs (*see also p112 and p140*).

John Wakelin Son of Edward Wakelin (*see above*) and apprenticed to him in 1766. He became a freeman in 1779. Registered marks with William Taylor in 1776 and 1777; registered mark in partnership with Robert Garrard in 1792.

James Wakley & Frank Clarke Wheeler Late 19th-century silversmiths who worked for Henry John Lias & Son. Registered marks in 1896 and 1906.

Joseph Walker Prominent early 18th-century Dublin maker of dishes, salvers and communion plate.

Matthew Walker Mid-18th-century Dublin maker of good-quality tablewares.

Thomas Walker Prominent early 18th-century Dublin maker. Registered three marks, all showing initials surmounted by a crown.

Walker & Hall Sheffield-based gold and silver workers founded in 1843, initially specializing in electroplate. Sir John Bingham, Hall's nephew, joined and ran the company until his death in 1916, when he was succeeded by Sir Albert Bingham. They registered marks as gold and silver workers in 1903, 1906, 1907 and 1913. The firm had branches throughout the UK. In 1971 they became part of Mappin & Webb, later British Silverware Limited.

 Thomas Wallis Apprenticed to Thomas Wallis snr. Registered marks in 1778; four between 1780–89, and two more in 1792 and 1810 (the last in partnership with Jonathan Hayne).

 Matthew Walsh Late 18th-century Dublin maker of good-quality tablewares.

 Michael Walsh Late 18th-century Dublin maker of good quality candlesticks and other wares.

 Joseph Ward Apprenticed to Joseph Slicer. Marks registered *c.*1697 and 1717.

 Benjamin Watts Spoonmaker; apprenticed to Walter Bradley in 1691. Registered marks date from 1698 and 1720.

 Richard Watts Apprenticed to Christopher Canner. Registered two marks in 1710 and a further one in 1720.

 Weir & Rogers Late 19th-century Dublin retailers of silverwares.

 Samuel Welder Maker of domestic hollow wares, especially casters. Apprenticed to Robert Keble in 1707; became a freeman in 1714. Registered marks date from 1714, 1717, 1720 and 1729.

 Benjamin West Apprenticed to James Smith in 1725; became a freeman in 1733. Registered marks in 1738 and 1739.

 Alderman West & Co Renowned 19th-century Dublin retailer of a wide range of fine-quality silverware.

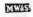 **M. West & Sons** Top 19th-century Dublin retailer of fine-quality silverware.

 William West Apprenticed to William Wildboar in 1735. Registered mark in 1738.

 Gervase Wheeler London agent for the well-known Birmingham jewellers, Ledsam, Vale & Wheeler. Registered a mark in 1818 which is often seen on silver boxes.

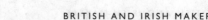

Thomas Whipham Apprenticed to Thomas Farren in 1728. Registered marks in 1737, 1739 (in partnership with William Williams), 1740, and 1757 (in partnership with Charles Wright). Liveried in 1746.

Fuller White & John Fray Mid-18th-century makers of medium-quality domestic wares such as cups and coffee-pots. Registered mark in 1745. Partnership had dissolved by 1748 when Fray registered a separate mark.

Samuel & George Whitford Registered only mark in partnership with Samuel in 1802. Partnership dissolved later the same year, when Samuel recorded the first of several separate marks.

Christopher & Thomas Wilkes Barker Thomas was the son of Christopher and apprenticed to William Fearn in 1787. Registered marks in partnership in 1800 and 1804; partnership dissolved by 1805 when Thomas entered a mark alone.

Denis Wilks Registered marks in 1737, 1739, 1747 and in 1753 in partnership with John Fray. The partnership had dissolved in 1756, when Fray entered his own mark.

James Wilks Registered marks in 1722, *c.*1728, 1739 and 1742.

David Willaume snr Important Huguenot silversmith. Marks registered *c.*1697, 1719 and 1720. Daughter Anne married David Tanqueray (*see p149*). Patronized by many of the most wealthy members of the aristocracy.

David Willaume jnr Apprenticed to his father, David (*see above*). Registered marks in 1728 and 1739.

William Williamson Mid-18th-century Dublin maker of fine-quality silverwares.

James Willmott Registered his only mark in 1741.

Thomas Wimbush Registered mark in 1828 and in partnership with Henry Hyde in 1834.

Samuel Wintle Mark registered, in 1778, in partnership with Thomas Wintle, as bucklemakers from 2 Blue Coat Building, Butcher Hall Lane. Other marks registered alone date from 1779, 1783 (as a smallworker) and 1792.

 Edward Wood Specialist maker of salts. Apprenticed to James Roode in 1715; became a freeman in 1722. Registered marks in 1722, 1735 and 1740. David Hennell served as his apprentice in 1728.

 Samuel Wood Specialist caster and cruet maker. Apprenticed to Thomas Bamford in 1721; became a freeman in 1730. Registered marks in 1733, c.1737, 1739, 1754 and 1756.

 Christopher Woods Registered mark in 1775 as a plateworker from King Street, St Ann's.

 William Woodward Apprenticed to William Pearson in 1719 and to George Wickes in 1722; became a freeman in 1726. Registered marks in 1731 and 1743.

 Charles Wright Apprenticed to Thomas Whipham in 1747; became a freeman in 1754. Registered mark in partnership with Whipham in 1757. Further marks registered alone in 1775 and 1780. Liveried in 1758; became a member of Court in 1777 and a Warden from 1783 to 1785. Died in 1815.

 John Yapp & John Woodward Registered mark as plateworkers in 1846. They had a manufactory at 13 Bread Street, Birmingham and a warehouse at 11 Thamvies Inn.

 James Young Late 18th-century maker of neo-classical silverwares. Registered mark in 1774 in partnership with Orlando Jackson and alone in 1775.

John Younge & Company Late 18th–early 19th-century Sheffield maker of candlesticks and other wares.

 Richard Zouch Apprenticed to Francis Plymley in 1720 and William Darker in 1735; became a freeman in 1737. Registered marks in 1735 and 1739.

Henry Auguste Paris silversmith, born 1759, son of Robert-Joseph (*see below*). Master 1785. Made large impressive tablewares in Empire style, including soup tureens, bowls on stands, ewers, caskets. Died 1816.

Robert Joseph Auguste Paris silversmith, born *c.*1730, master 1757. Father of Henry Auguste (*see above*). Wares include wine coolers, candlesticks, soup tureens, dinner plates. Many pieces made to royal commission; royal clients included Catherine the Great and George III. Died 1805.

Melchior Bair Augsburg silversmith, born *c.*1550, master 1576. Made parcel gilt standing cups in form of fruit. Mark also recorded on wager cups and salts. Died 1634.

Edmé-Pierre Balzac Paris silversmith, master 1739. Brother of Jean François Balzac, who was also a prominent silversmith. Mark recorded on covered dishes, candlesticks, flatware and wine coolers. Died *c.*1780.

Nicholas Besnier Paris silversmith, master 1714. Silversmith to King Louis XV. Royal commissions included a basin for the Spanish fiancée of the King. Besnier's daughter married Jacques Roettiers (*see below*). Died 1754.

Biennais

Martin Guillaume Biennais Paris silversmith born 1764. Established a workshop by *c.*1790; became official goldsmith to Napoleon. Made a wide variety of wares including necessaires, salvers, tureens, ewers. Retired 1819, died 1843.

Albrecht Biller Augsburg silversmith, born 1653. Mark recorded on a variety of small wares, including beakers, cups, and toilet set. Died 1720.

Johann Jakob Biller II Augsburg silversmith, born 1715. Mark recorded on candlesticks, dishes and beakers. Died 1777.

Thomas Boogaert Born Utrecht, where he served apprenticeship. Became master

1625; worked in Amsterdam. Mark recorded on salts and a tazza. Died 1653.

 Daniel Bouman Amsterdam silversmith, born 1644. Specialized in teapots and sugar bowls. Died 1692.

 Reynier Brandt Amsterdam silversmith, born 1702, master 1734. Made pierced baskets, tea wares, and salvers. Died 1788.

 Esaias Busch III Augsburg silversmith, born 1676. Mark recorded on a variety of hollow ware including teapots, dishes, caddies and boxes. Died 1759.

 Joseph-Pierre-Jacques Duguay Paris silversmith, born 1724, master 1756. Made ewers and basins, cruets and other table wares. Died 1749.

 Johann Jakob Dulliker Swiss silversmith working in Berne, born 1731. Mark recorded on bowls and caddies. Died 1810.

 Franssoys Eelioet Utrecht silversmith, born *c.*1585. Mark, recorded on standing cup, shows stag's antlers. Died 1642.

 Francois-Thomas Germain Paris silversmith, born 1726, son of Thomas Germain, grandson of Pierre Germain. Took over family business in 1748 as royal silversmith. Commissions included centrepieces for Empress Elizabeth of Russia, and a toilet service for the King of Portugal. Became bankrupt in 1765. Died 1791.

 Pierre Germain (le Roman) Born 1716, master 1744. Not known to have been related to more famous Germains. Apprenticed in 1736 to Nicolas Besnier. Published a famous book of designs *"Elements d'Orfèvrerie"* in 1748. Died 1783.

 Thomas Germain Paris silversmith, born 1673, eldest of 7 children of Pierre. Became silversmith to King Louis XV, also made pieces for King of Portugal, Queen of Spain, wife of Philip V. Died 1748.

 Louis-Joseph Lehendrick Paris silversmith, served apprenticeship under Thomas Germain (*see above*) master 1745. Mark recorded on candlesticks, dishes, coffee pots. Work notable for high-quality engraving and chasing and elegant design. Died 1783.

Alexis Loir III Paris silversmith, master 1733, mark recorded on dishes and candlesticks of high quality. Died 1775.

Jean-Baptiste-Claude Odiot Paris silversmith, born 1763, master 1785. Work included many large hollow wares including dishes, ewers, vases and bowls. Designs reflected Empire style with motifs such as leopards' heads, swans, rams' heads and classical masks. Died 1850.

Jean-Louis-Dieudonne Outrebon Paris silversmith, master 1772. Made high-quality plate and hollow wares, including ewers, dishes, coffee pots and candlesticks.

Jan Diederik Pont Amsterdam silversmith, born 1702, master 1729. Made variety of small wares including miniature sauceboats, candlesticks snuffers, boxes. Died 1767.

Hendrik Niewenhuys Amsterdam silversmith, born 1742, master 1763. Made variety of hollow wares including sauce tureens, teapots, boxes. Died 1803.

Ritter family Renowned Nuremburg family of silversmiths whose members included Christoff Ritter I (master 1547), Christoff Ritter II (master 1577), Wolff Christoff Ritter (master 1617), and Jeremias Ritter (master 1605).

Jacques Roettiers Paris silversmith, born 1707, master 1733. Son-in-law of Nicholas Besnier (*see above*), whose business he ran on his father-in-law's retirement. Father of Jacques Nicolas Roettiers (*see below*). Roettiers designed and managed a sizeable workshop. Notable commissions include the Berkeley Castle service, probably made for Augustus, son of 3rd Earl of Berkeley. Died 1784.

Jacques-Nicolas Roettiers Paris silversmith, born 1736. Son of Jacques Roettiers; took over his father's business on his retirement in 1772; master 1765. Commissions included a

3,000 piece service ordered by Catherine the Great in 1770 as a gift for Prince Gregory Orloff. Roettiers retired *c.*1777.

 Johannes Schiotling Amsterdam silversmith, born 1730, master 1762. Made a variety of wares such as cruets, boxes, tea wares and trays, often decorated with classical motifs such as garlands and swags. Died 1799.

 Jan Smit Amsterdam silversmith, born 1741, master 1769. Made candlesticks, teawares, sugar bowls. Died 1796.

 Frederik van Strant II Amsterdam silversmith, born 1709, master 1727. Made miniature tea wares. Nephew of Willem van Strant (*see below*). Died *c.*1750.

 Willem van Strant Amsterdam silversmith, born 1682, master 1727. Renowned for his miniature tea wares. Uncle of Frederik van Strant II (*see above*). Died 1742.

 Johann Andreas Thellott Augsburg silversmith, born 1655. Renowned for works decorated with elaborate chased relief scenes of mythological or historical subjects. Works include tankards, plaques and sweetmeat dishes. Died 1734.

 Etienne Terroux Geneva-based silversmith working *c.*1719. Formed partnership with son Jacques. Mark recorded on coffee pots, candlesticks and salvers. Died 1774.

 Christian Van Vianen Born *c.*1600 in Utrecht, son of Adam van Vianen. Settled in London, where he was employed by Charles I in the decoration of St George's Chapel, Windsor. Made tazzas and dishes which were typically elaborately chased and decorated. Died in London *c.*1667.

 Jan de Vries Amsterdam silversmith, born 1686, master 1710. Made tea wares. Died 1753.

 Wiener Werkstätte Viennese Workshops established 1903. Association of artist-craftsmen designers included Josef Hoffmann and Koloman Moser. Made a wide variety of objects intended to combine aesthetics with utility.

OTHER CONTINENTAL MAKERS

Allain, Henry, Paris, active *c.*1745, died *c.*1760.

Allen, Jacques-Louis, Paris, active *c.*1758, died 1783.

André, David, Paris, active *c.*1703.

Andrieux, Jean-Baptiste, Paris, active *c.*1830.

Anthiaume, Jacques, Paris, active mid-18thC.

Anthiaume, Louis-Julien, Paris, active *c.*1780-1790.

Aucoc, André, Paris manufacturer founded 1821.

Balaine, Charles, Paris, active *c.*1830.

Bailly, Antoine, Paris, active *c.*1750, died 1765.

Bair, Paulus, Nuremberg, active 1613.

Ballin, Claude, Paris, active *c.*1688, died 1754.

Balzac, Jean-François, Paris, active *c.*1749, died *c.*1765.

Barde, Jean-Daniel, Geneva, born 1705, active *c.*1730-1740, died 1780.

Barry, Thomas-Michel, Paris, active *c.*1800.

Bartermann, Johann I, Augsburg, born 1661, active 1690-1700, died 1732.

Bastier, Jean, Paris, active *c.*1764, died 1711.

Bataille, Charles-Nicolas, Paris, active *c.*1740, died 1759.

Baube, Jean Baptiste, Tours, active *c.*1725-1765.

Baur, Matthäus II, Augsburg, active 1680-1690, died 1728.

Bellanger, Joseph, Paris, active *c.*1725.

Bellanger, Louis, Paris, active *c.*1720, died 1755.

Belleville, Pierre, Montpellier, active 1736, died 1765.

Belli, Pietro, Rome, born *c.*1780, active *c.*1825, died 1828.

Berger, Louis-Jacques, Paris, active *c.*1805.

Berthe, Julien, Paris, active *c.*1722-1755.

Berthet, Jean-Baptiste-François, Paris, active early 19thC.

Bertin, Jean-Baptiste, Paris, active *c.*1740, died 1771.

Bertin, Nicholas, Paris, active *c.*1700.

Bertrand, Jean-Louis, Metz, active *c.*1735-45.

Besnier, Jacques, Paris, active *c.*1720, died 1761.

Beydel, Jacques Laurent, Paris, active *c.*1795.

Bibron, Jean-Pierre, Paris, active *c.*1800.

Biller, Albrecht, Augsburg, born 1653, active 1680-1718, died 1720.

Biller, Johann Baptist, Augsburg, active 1637, died 1683.

Biller, Johan Jakob II, Augsburg, born 1715, active *c.*1740-1770, died 1777.

Biller, Johann Ludwig I, Augsburg, born 1658, active 1684-1705, died 1732.

Böhm, Hermann, Vienna, active 19th century.

Boullier, Antoine, Paris, active *c.*1775-1805.

Bourgeois, Charles-Louis, Paris, active *c.* 1800.

Boutheroue-Desmarais, César Charles, Paris, active *c.*1730, died 1758.

Bugatti, Carlo, Italian designer, born 1855, died 1940.

Bunsen, Frantz Peter, Hanover, born 1725, active *c.*1790.

Busch, Esias I, Augsburg, active 1632, died 1679.

Cahier, Jean-Charles, Paris, born 1772, active first half 19thC.

Cardeilhac, Paris manufacturer, founded 1802.

Carron, Jean-François, Paris, active *c.*1755-1800.

Cartier, Paris manufacturer, founded 1859.

Charvet, Joseph, Paris, active *c.*1750-60.

Chayé, Germain, Paris, active *c.*1755.

Chéret, Jean-Baptiste-François, Paris, active *c.*1760.

Chéret, Pierre-Henry, Paris, active *c.*1740, died 1787.

Christofle & Cie, Paris manufacturer, founded 1805.

Cortelazzo, Antonio, Vicenza, born 1819, active mid-19thC.

Cousinet, Henry-Nicholas, Paris, active *c.*1725, died 1768.

Crose,Charles-François, Paris, active *c.*1715.

Drentwett, Abraham II, Augsburg, born 1647, active *c.*1675-1700, died 1729.

Drentwett, Christian II, Augsburg, born 1729, active *c.*1755-1780, died 1801.

Drentwett, Emanuel Abraham, Augsburg, born 1723, active *c.*1750, died 1770.

Drentwett, Gottlieb Christian, Augsburg, active *c.*1750, died 1754.

Durand, Antoine Sebastien, Paris, active *c.*1740.

Durand, François, Paris, active *c.*1830-1870.

Erhlen, Jean-Jacques, Strasbourg, active *c.*1730.

Eckloff, Paul, Königsberg, active 1612.

Fabergé, Peter Carl, St Petersburg and Moscow, born 1846, firm closed in 1918.

Fauche, Jean, Paris, active *c.*1735.

Ferrier, René Pierre, Paris, active *c.*1775.

Filassier, Antoine, Paris, active *c.*1705.

Filassier, Jacques, Paris, active *c.*1718.

Giannotti, Angelo, Rome, born 1798, active *c.*1825, died 1865.

Giraud, Jacques-Joseph I, Marseille, active *c.*1705-1750.

Girschner, Johann Christian, Augsburg, active *c.*1740-1765, died 1772.

Gouel, Gilles-Claude, Paris, active *c.*1730, died 1769.

Haan, Cornelis de, The Hague, born 1735, active *c.*1755-1780, died 1788.

Haan, Marcelus de, The Hague, born 1707, active *c.*1730-1740, died 1790.

Hallberg , C. G., Stockholm, active 1908.

Haydt, Balthasar, Augsburg, active 1645, died 1680.

Heckell, Michael II, Augsburg, active *c.*1720, died 1726.

Heckenauer, Johann Philipp, Augsburg, born 1705, active *c.*1740-60, died 1793.

Herminotte, Joannes Andreas I, Maastricht, active *c.*1760-70.

Erhard, Johann II, Augsburg, active *c.*1720-30, died 1757.

Heuglin, Martin II, Augsburg, active 1670, died 1675.

Ingermann, Christian Heinrich, Dresden, active *c.*1730-50.

Huguet, Jean-Vincent, Paris, active *c.*1745.

Igonet, Sébastien, Paris, active *c.*1725.

Imlin, Jean-Louis II, Strasbourg, active *c.*1720, died 1764.

Ivanov, Peter, Moscow, active *c.*1685–1710.

Jensen, Georg, Copenhagen, born 1866, founded
workshop 1904. Died 1935.

Johnsen, Niels, Copenhagen, active *c.*1720-40.

Keen, Pieter de, Amsterdam, born 1659,
active *c.*1680–1733, died 1742.

Kilb, Jakob Wilhelm, Augsburg, active *c.*1770-80,
died 1782.

Klinge, J., Breslau, active *c.*1700-30, died 1737.

Klinkosch, J. C.,Vienna retailer founded 1797.

Klosse, Johann Georg, Augsburg, active *c.*1738–1765,
died 1766.

Kopping, Johann Fredrik, St Petersburg, active *c.*1750,
died 1783.

Kramer, Tobias, Augsburg, active 1613, died 1634.

Lakomkin, G., Moscow, active *c.*1735-55.

Lambrecht, Hinrich, Hamburg, active 1610, died 1628.

Langlois, Nicolas Martin, Paris, active *c.*1757.

Michelson, Anton, Copenhagen, born 1809,
active *c.*1840, died 1877.

Michelson, Carl, Copenhagen, continued family business
from 1877.

Lalique, René, Paris manufacturer born 1860, died 1945.

Lemon, Erik, Uppsala, born 1732, active *c.*1760-1800.

Lemoine, Alexandre Nicolas, Paris, active *c.*1766.

Mannlich, Heinrich, Augsburg, active 1660-70,
died 1698.

Mittnacht, Johann III, Augsburg, born 1706,
active 1735-55, died 1758.

Möllenborg, Gustav, Stockholm, active *c.*1897.

Morel, Jean-Valentin, Paris, born 1794, active *c.*1830,
died 1860.

Moulineau, Claude-Alexis, Paris, active *c.*1720,
died *c.*1750.

Niewenhuys, Hendrik, Amsterdam, born 1742,
active *c.*1760-80, died 1803.

Outrebon, Nicholas II, Paris, active *c.*1735, died 1779.

Ovchinnikov, Moscow manufacturer, founded 1853.

Pepfenhauser, Johann II, Augsburg, born 1666,
active 1690-1720, died 1754.

Pontus, Pierre Joseph, Lille, born 1723, active *c.*1745,
died 1784.

Poppe, Cornelius, Augsburg, active 1690-1705,
died 1723.

Puiforcat, Jean, Paris manufacturer 1897-1945.

Regnard, Louis, Paris, active *c.*1733, died 1779.

Reimers the Elder, Johannes Johannessen, Bergen,
active from *c.*1660-1710.

Rehfus, Georg Adam, Berne, borne 1784,
active *c.*1805-25, died 1858.

Riel, Reinhold, Nuremberg, active 1652, died *c.*1685.

Rigal, François, Paris, active *c.*1769, died 1788.

Rigal, Nicolas, Paris, active *c*.1745, died 1790.

Rohde, Peter II, Danzig, acitve 1650, died *c*.1675.

Satzger, Gottlieb, Augsburg, active *c*.1745-60, died 1783.

Schaller, Matthäus, Augsburg, active 1607, died 1652.

Schlaubitz, Nathaniel, Danzig, active 1690-1700, died 1726.

Simoli, Giuseppe, Naples, active *c*.1700.

Solanier, Paul, Augsburg, born 1635, active 1680-1720, died 1724.

Sondagh, Rudolph, Rotterdam, born 1726, active *c*.1745-1800, died 1812.

Spickerman, Johann Nikolaus, Augsburg, active *c*.1740-45, died 1747.

Stapele, François van, The Hague, active *c*.1720-60, died 1773.

Stapele, Martinus van, The Hague, born 1731, active *c*.1757-90, died 1806.

Stoer the Younger, Thomas, Nuremberg, active 1629, died *c*.1655.

Strant, Frederik van II, Amsterdam, born 1709, active *c*.1730-40, died *c*.1750.

Straub, Heinrich, Nuremburg, active 1608, died 1636.

Treffler, Johann Christoph I, Augsburg, active 1680-1700, died 1722.

Trioullier,C., Active *c*.1830.

Tuillier, Jacques, The Hague, active *c*.1700-20.

Valadier, Giuseppe, Rome, born 1762, active 1785, died 1817.

Valadier, Luigi, Rome, born 1726, active *c*.1760, died 1785.

Vallières, Nicolas-Clement, Paris, active *c*.1735-75.

Villeclair, Antoine-Jean de, Paris, active *c*.1750, died 1764.

Weiss, Georg Daniel, Nuremburg, active 1705-15.

Weiss, Nicholaus, Nuremberg, born 1544, active 1613, died 1631.

Wennerwall, Johann, Gothenburg, active *c*.1740, died 1768.

Weye, Bernhard Heinrich, Augsburg, active *c*.1735-65, died 1782.

Winter, Christian, Augsburg, born 1661, active 1690-1730, died 1737.

Wiber, Peter, Nuremberg, active 1603, died 1641.

Wolff, Bernt, Nijmegen, active *c*.1710.

AMERICAN MAKERS

There was no American equivalent to the comprehensive English hallmarking system, although some American-made pieces may bear State marks (the State of Connecticut, for example, is represented by a staff and three bunches of grapes, a motif which was originally engraved by John Coney for Connecticut's Colonial currency in 1702). Most American silver is, however, marked with a maker or retailer's mark. Unlike English makers' marks, where initials are nearly always used, many American makers marked their wares with their whole name which was placed within a simple decorative border, and these are usually relatively easily to identify. More recently-made silver may bear the retailer's mark. Listed below are the names and marks of a selection of leading American silversmiths and retailers. Other important makers are listed on pp164–5. Where precise birth/death dates are unavailable the dates given indicate the years in which the maker is believed to have been active.

PRINCIPAL AMERICAN MAKERS

Jeremiah Dummer (1645-1718)
Credited with being the first American-born silversmith. Served his apprenticeship with John Hull in Boston, and later engraving plates for Connecticut's first paper money. Made a large variety of silverwares, many of which survive today. Believed to have introduced gadrooning (*see p88*) to American silver *c*.1680.

Gorham Manufacturing Co. (1818-present day)
One of America's most prolific manufacturers of silverware. Company founded by Jabez Gorham (1792-1869) in Providence, Rhode Island. From *c*.1841 mechanical methods of manufacturing increasingly used. In 1868 firm joined by T. J. Pairpont and began marking their products with both a date and trade mark. Earlier silver predominantly influenced by 18th-century French styles; later Art Nouveau and Art Deco styles were adopted.

Paul Revere jnr (1735-1818)
Son of Huguenot silversmith, Paul Revere snr. Renowned for prodigious output and varied life. Dramatic ride to Lexington during the American War of Independence on 19 April 1775 was the subject of a poem by Longfellow. Prior to War of Independence, most of Revere's silverwares followed simple Georgian styles; later work reflected influence of English Regency designs.

Robert Sanderson (1608-93) After serving apprenticeship with William Rawlins of London for 9 years, Sanderson emigrated to America c.1640 and settled in Boston, Mass., where along with John Hull (1624-83), he was one of first recorded silversmiths to work in America. Much of his surviving work is ecclesiastical plate.

Tiffany Co (1837-present day) Company founded by Charles Louis Tiffany (1812-1902) and became one of America's largest, most prestigious silver manufacturers. Tiffany opened branch in Paris in 1853 and won an award at the Paris Exhibition of 1867. Among Tiffany's illustrious clientele were Queen Victoria, the Tsar of Russia and the Shah of Persia. The firm also made a large selection of good-quality household wares; from the 1890s they also began to produce electroplated wares.

OTHER AMERICAN MAKERS

Anthony, Joseph, Jr, Philadelphia, Pa., b.1762, d.1814
Austin, Josiah, Charlestown or Boston, Mass., c.1760-70
Ball, Black & Co., New York., c.1850-75
Ball, Tompkins & Black, New York., c.1840-50
Bard, Conrad, Philadelphia, Pa., c.1825-50
Bartlett, Samuel, Concord or Boston, Mass., b.1750, d.1821
Bigelow & Bros, Boston, Mass. c.1840-50
Casey, Samuel, South Kingston, R.I., c.1753-55
Clark, F. H. & Co., Memphis, Tenn., c.1850-55
Coburn, John, Boston, Mass., b.1725, d.1803
Dubois, Tunis, D., New York., c.1797-99
Edwards, Samuel, Boston, Mass., c.1728-30
Emery, Stephen, Boston, Mass., b.1725, d.1801
Faris, Charles, Annapolis, Md., c.1785-1800
Faris, Hyram, Annapolis, Md., c.1790-1800
Faris, William Jr., Annapolis Md; Norfolk Va; Havana, Cuba; Edenton, N.C., 1782-1803
Forbes, John, W., New York, 1810-40
Forbes, William, New York, c.1775-1830
Fueter, Daniel C., New York, c.1755-1805
Gale, William & Son, New York, c.1825-50
Gardiner, Baldwin, Philadelphia, Pa., New York, c.1815-40
Gelston & Treadwell, New York, c.1835-8
Gilbert, William, New York, c.1775-1818

Gregg, Hayden & Co., Charleston, S.C., c.1845-52

Hammersly, Thomas, New York., b.1727, d.1781

Harding, Newell, Haverhill and Boston, Mass., b.1796, d.1862

Hastier, John, New York, d.1791

Haverstick, William, Lancaster and Philaelphia, PA., c.1780-98

Henchman, Daniel, Boston, Mass., b.1730, d.1775

Heyer, William B., and Gale, Jesse, New York, c.1800-07

Hollingshead, William, Philadelphia, Pa., c.1755-85

Holmes, (Homes), William, Boston, Mass., b.1742, d.1825

Jacobi, A., Baltimore, Md., c.1878-80

Jones, Ball & Co., Boston, Mass., c.1850-52

Keyworth, Robert, Washington DC., c.1830-33

Kirk Samuel & Sons, Baltimore Md., 1845-60

Krider, Peter L., Philadelphia, Pa., c.1850-52

Lansing, Jacob, Albany, New York, 1681-1715

Le Roux, Bartholomew, New York, b.1681, d.1767

Lincoln & Foss, Boston, Mass., c.1850-2

Lownes, Joseph, Philadelphia, Pa., b.1754, d.1816

McMullin, John, Philadelphia, Pa., b.1765, d.1843

Marquand & Co., New York, c.1835-40

Monell & Williams, New York, c.1835-40

Moore, John, C., New York, c.1832-40

Musgrave, James, Philadelphia, Pa., c.1793-1812

Otis, Jonathan, Newport, R.I., c.1778-80

Owen, John, Jr, Philadelphia, Pa., c.1804-30

Pairpont Manfacturing Co., New Bedford, Mass., 1880-present

Revere, Paul, Sr, Boston, Mass., c.1702-54

Rich, Obadiah, Boston, Mass., c.1830-50

Richarson, Joseph, Philadelphia, Pa., 1711-85

Schanck, John, A., New York, c.1792-7

Shreve, Brown & Co., Boston, Mass., c.1856-8

Stacy, Philemon, Jr, Boston, Mass., b.1704, d.1750

Starr, Theodore, B., New York, c.1900

Syng, Philip, Jr, Philadelphia, Pa., b.1703, d.1789

Targee, John & Peter, New York, c.1798-1810

Ten Eyck, Barent, Albany, N.Y., b.1714, d.1793

Ten Eyck, Koenraet, Albany, N.Y., c.1703-50

Thomson, William, New York, c.1810-35

Waterman, New York, c.1835

R. Wallace & Co., Wallingford, Conn., c.1854-6

Wilcox & Evertson, New York, c.1892-8

Wilson, R & W., Philadelphia, Pa., c.1825-45

Wiltberger, Christian, Philadelphia, Pa., b.1766, d.1851

Wishart, Hugh, New York, c.1785-1820

Wood & Hughes, New York, c.1845-8

GOLD HALLMARKING

Like silver, gold is alloyed in order to harden it. Silver and copper are the main alloys, sometimes used in combination. The alloy will determine the colour of the final metal. Gold alloyed with nickel, for example, will be whiter in tone, whilst a copper alloy will produce a yellower metal.

The standard marks for sterling silver and gold were the same until 1798. In 1300, Edward I laid down the first legal standard of gold as equal to the "Touch of Paris", or 19⅕ carats of pure gold to 24, a carat being the 24th part weight of the whole – i.e. an item of gold had to contain a minimum of 19⅕ parts of pure gold per 24. Like the first silver hallmark laid down at the same time, this standard was acknowledged with the leopard's head (*see pp6-17*). The maker's mark was required from 1363 and a date letter was added in 1578. In 1477 the standard was reduced to 18 carats, which lasted until 1575 when it became 22 carats, a standard that still applies today. From 1544 the standard mark was altered to a lion *passant*. When the lower 18 carat standard was readmitted as a legal standard in 1798 it was shown by a crown mark; this remained until 1844 when the crown mark came to be used for both standards. In 1854 three more standards were established – 15 carat, 12 carat and 9 carat – and from this time the specific quality was indicated by both a figure and a percentage. Finally, in 1932, the 12 and 15 carat standards were dropped and replaced by the 14 carat standard.

One short-lived mark was the sun, used on 22 carat gold assayed in London between 29 May 1816 and the introduction of the crown in 1844.

STANDARD MARK

	To 1974	1975-present	foreign imports
22 carat	🛡️ 22	👑 916	☀️ 916
18 carat	🛡️ 18	👑 750	☀️ 750
14 carat	14 585	👑 585	☀️ 585
9 carat	9 375	👑 375	☀️ 375

Scottish offices used the following marks in the place of the crown:

Edinburgh	Glasgow
🦁	🦁 🌳

London	😀	Newcastle	🛡	Glasgow	🦅
Birmingham	⚓	Sheffield	🌹	Dublin	🧍
Chester	🛡	York	⊞		
Exeter	🏰	Edinburgh	🏰		

FOREIGN PIECES IMPORTED TO BRITAIN

From 1842 imported pieces were assayed and hall-marked. From 1876 the mark included a stamped "F". After 1904 each assay office was allocated a special office mark for foreign items to replace the normal office mark.

London	♋	Birmingham	△	Chester	▣
Sheffield	▤	Edinburgh	⊠	Glasgow	▣

PLATINUM HALLMARKING

Platinum did not come under hallmarking law until as recently as 1973, when the Hallmarking Act introduced a standard of 950 parts per thousand. With effect from 2 January 1975, all platinum wares made in Great Britain that meet this standard have been marked with an orb and cross set within a pentagon. Imported platinum wares bear the figure '950'.

orb date letter

imported mark

assay office marks

London   Birmingham   Sheffield

SHEFFIELD PLATE

The craft of covering a base metal with a precious metal, known as close plating, has been practised for centuries. The process involves the application of a thin sheet of, for example, silver, to a pre-formed vessel using heat and a hammer. The thickness of this sheet can be minute — the fact that silver can be beaten to a sheet 1/1000th of an inch thick, or drawn to a wire of that diameter gives an indication of its malleability. It was not until the mid-18th century that a commercially viable variation, which became known as Sheffield plate, allowed the large-scale production of plated wares for domestic use.

Sheffield plate was formed with thin sheets of silver and copper annealed together under pressure before being made into the required object. The secret of its success was that it could be used to produce a host of items, from the simplest button to the grandest epergne, at a fraction of the cost of a solid silver equivalent.

The development of Sheffield plate is said to have begun in the workshop of one Thomas Bolsover, a Sheffield cutler, whilst working to repair a knife, the handle of which was part copper, part silver. Bolsover found that under heat and pressure the copper and the silver became inseparable — and he began to use this new material to make small items such as buttons, buckles and novelty wares.

At this time there was considerable development in rolling mills and it was not long before small objects made from Sheffield plate were being manufactured on a large scale. The silver sheeting used was of sterling standard and therefore ideally suitable with its copper core to be raised in the same way as solid silver; and it is common to see hammer marks on the inside of Sheffield-plated coffee pots, tankards and mugs which were made in the 1770s.

The disadvantage of the malleability of Sheffield plate was that the silver and copper sandwich tended to "fray" at the edges in the course of production. To prevent this from happening and to solidify and mask the border where the copper core was visible, the edge could be cut at an angle and the outer skin of silver rolled over. Alternatively, a wire or thread border, rather like a miniature hosepipe was cut along its length and applied to the edge.

As fashions changed and designs became more elaborate (especially after 1800), borders of stylized foliate form became the vogue. In order to copy these the Sheffield plate worker stamped out the required pattern for rims, handles and feet in sterling silver and filled the cavities with lead to recreate the effect of a border on a solid silver piece. The filled borders would be applied to the body and secured with a rollover edge. Such rolled edges will be visually apparent as well as being identifiable by touch.

By 1824, Sheffield plate production techniques had advanced to such a degree that the rollover edge and wire became redundant.

Certain characteristics of Sheffield plate can help authentication. On a genuine piece of Sheffield plate, a solid silver plaque was often set into the surface where an engraving might be placed. A coat of arms, for example, would be unsightly if the engraver cut through to the layer of copper. Although the standard of silver of the skin and solid plate are the same, the plated area will become visible when breathed upon.

On less important pieces (and certainly on less expensive wares where the underside will not show), only the outer surface had a silver skin, the reverse being tinned. This was a common practice on snuffer trays, chamber candlesticks and the insides of less important pots and jugs.

As might be expected, the designs for Sheffield plate of any period closely followed those on contemporary sterling silver and changed just as rapidly. Therefore shape and decoration are contributory and important guides to dating. After the 1840s and the advent of electroplating, materials other than copper were used as the base body material, the most popular being nickel (a hard white alloy sometimes known as German silver). Britannia metal was also used, as were numerous other alloys which reflected the often impractical side of Victorian inventiveness.

France produced considerable quantities of plate, but their methods of manufacture did not change as rapidly as those in the United Kingdom. Slight differences in style and decoration are usually enough to indicate foreign origin. In England, the greatest areas of production have traditionally been Sheffield and Birmingham, the latter being home to one of the most famous Sheffield plate manufactories, the Soho works of Matthew Bolton. His distinctive mark, comprising two 8-pointed stars, can be found on, for example, candlesticks, epergnes and wine coolers of the finest quality.

Early Sheffield plate was rarely marked, if at all. In 1784 legislation was introduced that allowed for a maker's mark and device, a note of which was to be kept in a register maintained by the Sheffield Assay Office. The practice of marking became more common as the century progressed.

It was not until the late 18th century that a set of marks, almost pseudo-hallmarks, began to appear, which were dangerously similar to those applied to sterling silver. The Plate Assay (Sheffield and Birmingham) Act of 1772 ordered these two assay offices to ensure that no marks applied to plated goods should resemble those on silver too closely.

By the 1820s, makers marks often consisted of the name in full, split in two to fit a rectangular punch, although initials remained partly in use.

By the 1840s a crown, a *fleur-de-lys* and other confusing symbols were added, set in a straight line. During the second half of the 19th century the letters *E.P.N.S.* (electroplated nickel silver) and *E.P.B.M.* (electroplated Britannia metal) appeared, very often disguised, or set to appear at first sight like hallmarks. However, on closer inspection, there is little danger of confusing these substitutes with sterling silver or Sheffield plate.

Listed below are the names and marks of a selection of the most prominent and prolific makers of Sheffield plate.

BOULTON	M. Boulton & Co.
	C. G. Cope
	T. & J. Creswick
	J. Dixon & Sons
	T. Dixon & Co.
	W. Ellerby
	H. Freeth
	W. Garnett
	J. Gilbert
	W. Hall
	Joseph Hancock
	T. Harwood
	H. Holland & Co.
	S. & T. Howard

Hutton Ⓐ Hutton Ⓐ	W. Hutton
H & S ⬚	W. Hutton
R.LAW. ⬚	R. Law
A·CLEA ✕	A. C. Lea
J.LOVE·&·C⬚	J. Love & Co.
MERE DITH ⬚	H. Meredith
MOORE Ω	J. Moore
✝ ROBERTS	J. & S Roberts
⬚	Cadman Roberts & Co.
Sil- kirk?	W. Silkirk
⬚	Smith Robarts & Co.
H ⬚ ⬚ ⬚ ⬚	
𝒦 𝒯 & 𝒞ᵒ	Tudor & Leader
⬚ ⬚ ⬚ ⬚	Tudor & Leader
⬚	Hatfield Waterhouse & Co.
⬚	J. Watson & Son
DAN: HOLY WILKINSON & Cᵒ	D. Holy Wilkinson & Co.
WOOD WARD ✕ WOOD WARD ✕	W. Woodward
WRIGHT FAIRBAIRN	J. Wright & G. Fairburn
S.C.YOUNGE & Cᵒ	S. & C. Younge & Co.

FAKES AND ALTERATIONS

Despite the stringent application of hallmarks to English silver, collectors should be wary of faked and altered wares. All English wrought plate from the 17th, 18th and early 19th centuries, with the exception of very small pieces, should bear the requisite hallmarks, but examples of unmarked antique silver continue to emerge for a large variety of reasons. As from 1 January 1975 (in compliance with the 1973 Hallmarking Act), such pieces may be sold as silver if they were made before 1900 and have not since been altered in any way. However, if an article has had its essential character changed by alteration, for however innocent a reason, it may not legally be sold until the alteration has been regularized by an assay office. Providing all additional parts of a piece are hallmarked at the time of construction, the item will comply with the law. Hallmarks which have been forged, or moved from one piece to another are, however, illegal.

The faker of silver articles has to be much more inventive than fakers in other areas of antiques, as he has to produce not only the piece but also the hallmark. The silver hallmarking system is the oldest form of consumer protection, and the assay master the guardian of honest standards of practice.

The assay master also heads the Antique Plate Committee whose role it is to investigate suspicious wares put up for sale. In the unlikely event of a faked piece escaping the eye of the Antique Plate Committee and being sold at auction, the major auction houses, in order to protect their international reputations, offer a five-year guarantee which gives additional protection. Dissatisfied collectors are also protected by The Trade Descriptions Act.

Honest Replicas

As collecting silver became increasingly popular, makers saw a market for replica wares. Honest copying became a fashionable activity from the late 18th century, when several large manufacturing silversmiths, such as Garrards and Rundell, Bridge & Rundell, used the designs of the past for their inspiration and began reproducing late 17th-century Baroque-style and mid-18th-century rococo-style pieces. However, providing that a piece bears hallmarks contemporary with its production rather than the period of its style, then it may be termed an "honest replica" and is not illegal.

FAKING

There are three types of fake silver:

* articles with forged hallmarks
* articles with transposed hallmarks
* hallmarked pieces which have been altered or incorporated into others.

Thus fake silverware can be old and improved, or completely new and made to an antique pattern. Without the motives of tax evasion, or the added value of later alteration, the reasons for the out-of-period piece dating from the 17th or 18th century may be difficult to understand. If you come across such a piece, take it to an expert.

What To Look For

There are several crucial areas where evidence of faking may present itself. The detailing in the construction or decoration may be rather stiff, or the piece may lack the wear that could be expected of an antique. More importantly, look at the proportion; with a little experience collectors will be able to familiarize themselves with the proportions typical of each era of silver manufacture, enabling them to recognise a fake. For example, the bowl of a faked spoon may be too large for most genuine examples of their supposed period.

Forged Hallmarks

Forged hallmarks are applied to modern sterling silver to pass it off as antique, or to sub-standard metal to make it appear of quality. They can be created in any of three ways – by the use of faked punches, or by either casting or electrotyping a copy of a genuine piece, marks and all. Comparing marks known to be genuine with suspect ones was until recently a fail-safe method of detecting faked punches. However, forgers are becoming increasingly sophisticated and in certain cases microscopic examination is used to determine the authenticity of a dubious mark.

Transposed Hallmarks

Transposition involves the removal of a hallmark from a small piece, to be inserted into a larger, unassayed item — for example, the marks on the back of a spoon may be cut out and let into the neck of a coffee pot, the solder line often being disguised with *repoussé* decoration. Such a line may sometimes be made visible by frosting the surface, an effect commonly achieved by breathing on the piece of silver. (Metal is generally colder than breath and silver solder and any other imperfection becomes more apparent through the resulting condensation.) If the results are suspicious, consult an expert. Although marks are occasionally transposed from a genuine antique item to a modern piece, in order to fake age, the majority of examples seen today were applied in the 18th and 19th centuries by "duty dodgers" (*see p16*) to avoid the punitive duty placed on silver.

ALTERED WARES

A general interest in silver did not emerge until the latter part of the 19th century, hence the majority of silverware faked or altered for pecuniary gain dates from that period onwards. Before this time an article may have been altered for practical or aesthetic reasons, or because the owner could not afford the cost of remaking. During the 19th century there was the additional incentive of "bringing up to date" inherited plain silver. For example, during the 1850s countless 18th-century tankards were converted into jugs by the addition of a spout opposite the handle and the embossing of the baluster body and domed lid with a floral design (see p179).

The Scratchweight
Many items can be seen to bear a series of lightly engraved numbers, usually on the underside, which indicate the weight of the item at the time of assay – a small salver engraved 11.2 indicates that the article weighed 11 ounces and 2 pennyweights troy. These numbers enable us to establish whether or not anything has been added or taken away by simply weighing the piece on a pair of silver scales. Depending on the article, a small percentage of loss could be accounted for by cleaning, but the loss should not be great and the piece should certainly not be heavier.

Armorials
It has always been fashionable for families to engrave their coat of arms, crest or monogram within a decorative cartouche in a prominent place on a piece of silver, especially on larger items (see *Armorials and Cartouches pp86-7*). However, from the 1890s fashions changed and any inscription reduced the value of an article of silver (except in the cases where it referred to a prominent or royal personage or event) and it became commonplace to have such engraving erased by removing the engraved layer of silver. When fashion changed once more and armorials returned to favour, the arms of a new owner were engraved in the vacated space. During the 1920s the demand for plain, unascribed silver returned and sometimes a piece had its engraving removed for a second, or even a third time. If the silver became too thin as a result of the erasing, the upper surface was beaten back again and the resulting dip filled. Differences in colour were sometimes concealed by electroplating the new surface. Removed engravings may be detected by viewing the piece obliquely. If an armorial has been removed an irregular dip may be visible. There may also be a discernible variation in the overall colour. Another way of testing is to place a finger and thumb on opposite sides of the silver and move them towards the suspect area. If a layer has been removed a difference will be felt in the gauge of the silver.

Later Decoration
Many earlier pieces of silver were altered at a later date to make them more useful or more fashionable. In attempting to detect alteration, collectors should form

an initial impression based on style, and then ask themselves certain questions.

> 1. Is the piece fully marked?
> 2. Are the hallmarks consistent with the initial impression of date?
> 3. Are they distorted or in an unusual position?
> 4. Do any subsidiary pieces lack the correct marks?
> 5. Are there any signs of repair, such as patches or rough soldering, where separately-made pieces have been attached?

Candlesticks and Candelabra

Most early candlesticks, until *c.*1770, were made by using the cast method (*see pp81-5*). By using a genuine candlestick to make a mould, the unscrupulous maker can reproduce accurate cast replicas, including marks, of these with ease. The most important thing to remember is that genuine marks will have been struck individually and randomly and will never appear in precisely the same position on any two pieces.

Occasionally marks are removed from less valuable pieces of table silver and "let in" on the edge of the base of loaded candlesticks. Seams where the hallmark has been applied are usually visible, and the maker's mark will often be that of a spoonmaker.

Always examine candelabra carefully; the branches should be marked with date letter, standard, duty, town and maker's mark, depending on their period. Any detachable parts, such as a drip-pan or nozzle, should always be marked with the maker's and duty marks to match the stick. It is quite common to find candelabra with later branches because they were easily mislaid when large sets of candlesticks and candelabra were split up. Replica branches are acceptable provided they are marked accordingly.

Sometimes handles and feet were added to snuffers later. Snuffers are also occasionally transformed into inkstands: silver rings are added to the snuffer tray to form holders for glass inkwells. In such pieces there will be no marks on the added inkwell-holder.

Cow Creamers and Porringers

The vast majority of 18th-century cow creamers were made by John Schuppe in London between 1750 and 1775 (*see p145*). Dutch replicas were made from the 1880s onwards and are worth only a fraction of the price of earlier examples. Examples made in the 18th century are clearly identifiable from the hallmarks: if a cow-creamer is unmarked or has an unfamiliar mark it is almost certainly a later continental version and should be valued accordingly.

Porringers of an early 18th-century style are occasionally found made from later Georgian mugs and tankard lids. Such alterations may be detected by signs of distortion on the hallmarks.

Cream Jugs

In the past cream jugs or boats were often created by converting other less useful objects. Such alterations were not usually intended to deceive, merely to make a more desirable object from a redundant one. The most usual conversions were of caster to pitcher cream jug, and punch ladle or brandy saucepan bowl to small cream boat by adding handles and feet and reworking and spreading the lip. Familiarity with correct proportions is the best way of detecting such changes. The marks on conversions of this type may be obscured and when any alteration has involved the use of heat, the silver will have become discoloured.

A brandy saucepan with handle removed can be converted to a sugar basin or cream jug

Dishes and Plates

Simple circular dinner plates, soup plates and meat dishes, were produced in substantial numbers throughout the first half of the 18th century. After *c.*1740, as more elaborate plates with scrolled outlines and gadroon borders became fashionable, many plain services were updated. Plates which were not re-marked are discernible by the distortion apparent in the original marks. Some marks may also have been lost.

During the last century silver dinner plates have often been re-hammered into rose bowls and strawberry dishes. As with other types of alteration, distorted marks will give this away. Occasionally, soup plates were converted into dinner plates by removing the centre of the plate, cutting it down, re-hammering and soldering back into the border. These reworkings can be difficult to identify although an original scratchweight (*see p174*) may provide one way of checking. Soup plates are usually between 7½% and 15% heavier than dinner plates.

Sauce Boats and Tureens

Look out for let in marks on pedestal feet, and make sure a full set of marks appears – otherwise the piece may be a converted liner. Soup tureens made between 1805 and 1840 often had detachable liners, which should have the same set of marks as the tureen except that the town mark (leopard's head or mask in the case of London) will have been omitted.

The faker has in the past found a variety of uses for both the tureen liner and the wine cooler liner. Whilst the former can be turned into baskets, bowls or tureens, the latter can, by the addition of lids, become biscuit barrels or ice buckets.

Salvers and Trays

Faked tea trays are very unusual; however, when examining a piece pay careful attention to the mark. One which is distorted or struck unusually close to the border may be a sign that the tray has been reshaped or had additions to the borders. Occasionally, tea trays are created from oval salvers or meat dishes to which handles and feet have been added; such handles will usually not match the design of the border as they would on a genuine piece.

Plain Georgian salvers were sometimes converted into presentation pieces during the 19th century. If an inscription does not coincide with the mark, or if the style of decoration is not compatible with the date of the salver, then check carefully to see if there are any odd creases or seams which might denote an added border and/or feet. On salvers with borders added at a later date, the additions should have been hallmarked when they were applied, but such marks may be very small and hard to discern.

Tazzas (a type of salver on a raised central foot) were highly fashionable during the late 17th–early 18th century. When such pieces were no longer sought-after it was commonplace to remove their central feet and add three or four feet near the borders to convert them into salvers. Such pieces may be spotted because the removed central foot may have left a discernible mark. Occasionally this conversion was reversed and a salver was transformed into a tazza. If the tazza is genuine it should be struck with the correct lion *passant* or leopard's head erased mark, unless it is a provincial or late example dating from *c.*1750 onwards.

Spoons and Other Table Silver

Although the ordinary spoon, knife and fork are comparatively free from a forger's attention, some of the more expensive rarities and specialist collecting fields are not.

Sought-after types of spoons, such as caddy spoons, have long been popular with collectors. Among the most frequently-seen silver fakes of spoons are marriages between Georgian teaspoon handles (with their marks) and later, elaborate bowls.

Although the conversion of table silver is illegal, it is not against the law to alter and match up patterns without adding extra metal or substantially changing the form. Fiddle pattern (*see p102*) is not as popular as Old English, so the former is sometimes converted into the latter. Old English pattern in turn is not as sought-after as the more decorative later forms of the same design and is sometimes reworked into Old English thread, Feather Edge and Beaded patterns.

From the early years of the 19th century the strawberry became a cultivated fruit, and from *c.*1850 onwards the Victorians were fond of presenting "berry" (strawberry) spoons. These were usually made from plain earlier spoons embossed with foliage, fruit or flowers. Many of these spoons are marked pre-1800. Unlike other types of later-decorated silver, the value of "berry" spoons is usually double that of plain spoons.

Sauce ladles have occasionally been treated in a similar fashion to spoons and they are sometimes pierced to form sugar sifters.

Among the most sought-after and most faked types of spoons are apostle spoons. These were coveted by collectors from the end of the 18th century. Apostle spoons were made over a period of two centuries. Most English-made examples date from the late 16th and 17th centuries. There are various types of fakes; the most frequently seen is where a plain 18th-century spoon is reworked. Close examination usually reveals a casting from an original.

Other finial spoons such as seal tops and slip tops, as well as lion sejants and maidenheads, are also highly sought-after and prone to faking. All such spoons should be carefully examined to see that they have not been altered. Look carefully at the way in which the terminal has been applied. On London spoons the join should be made with a "V" and on provincial spoons there should be a lap or "L" joint.

Sugar Basins, Argylls and Brandy Saucepans
Early sugar basins were generously proportioned because the unrefined sugar in common usage meant that large basins were required for storage. In later years, as sugar bowls became smaller, early basins were sometimes refashioned as small teapots, with the addition of handles, lids and spouts.

Tankards
By the late 19th century covered tankards became unfashionable and were frequently changed into jugs or coffee pots. Such conversions were often embellished

with Victorian-style decoration.

Teapots, Stands and Kettles

Teapots were rarely converted but were often updated by the addition of decoration, a new spout, finials and a handle. Tea kettles, like teapots, were often altered, but are not commonly faked. Coffee pots were sometimes changed into teapots at a later date. Such alterations may be detected by distortion of the hallmarks; tea, coffee and hot water urns are occasionally formed from a cup and cover to which is added a tap; alternatively, urns may be converted to cups by the removal of taps. The commonest give-away is a seam disguised with inappropriate chased decoration.

An 18th-century tankard with Victorian chased decoration and unhallmarked (illegal) fox finial

Wine Funnels

Nowadays, wine funnels are highly sought-after by collectors and rarely tampered with. However in the past they were subjected to various alterations. The bowls were used as tea-strainers. By blocking the perforations the bowl could be transformed into a sugar basin or salt cellar. If the spout was replaced by a pedestal foot it could metamorphose into a goblet. A shorter foot and a spout could form a milk jug.

A wine funnel could be converted into a tea strainer, a goblet or a milk jug

COLLECTING SILVER

When setting out to buy silver, first establish what you want. Are you looking for a particular mark, or a certain type of candlestick, for example? Decide on a period, a style or a shape you desire, and always have a second choice in reserve. Read all you can, especially any history about the item or its design. Then consult dealers and auctioneers. Seek their advice as to prices and availability. It may be at this stage that you have to be less ambitious, but try and get the best example in your price bracket; it is preferable to have a superb cream jug from the 1820s than to have one of the same price but of lesser quality from the 1770s, as quality will always maintain its appeal, and therefore its value.

A good place to start a collection is with spoons. Spoons have a long history – examples from as far back as the 17th century can still be found – and the myriad types available reflect changing styles throughout the important periods of our social development, as well as providing an ideal way of learning about hallmarks and the manufacture of silver. There is a tremendous variety of spoons from which to choose, from modest teaspoons, to serving and basting spoons.

An alternative is to collect silver of a particular period or style, or even from one specific year. Or you may wish to furnish, for example, a table or sideboard in an appropriate style. A further suggestion could be to collect the work of one maker. Whatever your approach, the most important single rule is to collect only that which gives you pleasure each and every time you look at it.

Remembering Hallmarks

When you are setting out to buy silver, there is a simple method by which to remember the date letter system. Select a letter that is easy to recall – perhaps the initial of your surname – and note its position in the cycle. For example, if you select the letter B, the date letter B was used in 1717, 1737, 1757 etc. – therefore every odd 7. As long as you can recognize the shield or background to a date letter, you can pinpoint the cycle and count from your letter to the relevant year without having to count through more than 20 years.

Caring For Silver

Silver should not be just looked at. It was made to be used and you should not be afraid to do so – silver is difficult to break, and a dent, in the hands of an expert, can easily be removed. But prevention is better than cure, and there are several ways in which to look after silver in order to make damage less likely.

Use it and wash it; never clean it with an abrasive powder or liquid, as this will, over the years, gradually wear away the surface. Tragically, a large amount of 18th century silverwares have had their definition severely impaired by overzealous butlers and cleaners of the 19th and 20th centuries, who ill-advisedly used abrasive cleaning agents in the continual attempt to keep their silver sparkling. If the silver is badly tarnished, seek expert advice before taking any drastic measures. More importantly, if silver is regularly washed with mild soapy water and a soft chamois it won't tarnish, but gradually attain a soft mellow look, referred to as a "skin" in silver parlance. Try to avoid putting too many pieces of, for example, a silver tea service, on the same shelf – one thing you need with silver is plenty of storage space.

Never put self-adhesive tape over the hallmarks in order to protect them – there are acids in such tape that do more harm than good. Similarly, and for the same reason, never group cutlery with rubber bands, nor store rubber bands inside a silver cup or beaker.

Empty or remove all salt from the proximity of silver when not in use. A grain of salt will burn the surface of silver as seriously as a cigarette will burn wood. Indeed, an open, full salt cellar, placed in a sideboard or cupboard, will cause enormous damage to any silver wares around it, as the salt will permeate the air and deposit itself on every surface.

Nothing graces a table more elegantly than a silver candlestick. However, never remove a candle stub with a sharp, pointed implement, as the silver surface can so easily be scratched. Simply pour a little hot water around the sconce and, as silver conducts heat very effectively, the stub will soon be soft enough to slip out easily. Drops of wax can be removed in the same way from the drip pans and bases.

Repairs

One of the most fortunate things about silver it that, unlike other types of antique, when dropped or carelessly treated it may dent, but rarely breaks. But just as it is unwise to attempt a do-it-yourself job on mending your own porcelain, so it is with silver, in getting dents out, filling a hole or mending a split. Never attempt to repair a piece yourself. Serious and illegal damage can result and, while the process may not be complicated, it requires workshop conditions and the knowledge of the expert. Generally, a simple repair can be easily executed.

When the metal does split, however, it has to be repaired with silver solder, which can potentially lead the owner or repairer into a legal mine field. Any addition to a piece of silver subsequent to its original manufacture requires examination by the Antique Plate Committee at Goldsmiths' Hall (see p172) before it may be sold as a genuine item of sterling silver. The silver solder necessary in such repairs is a lower standard metal than sterling silver, with a lower melting point, and can thus be recognized as the introduction to the piece of a baser metal. This does not mean, of course, that a simple repair to a teapot with a hole in the wrong place means heavy legislative procedures for its continued use. It is only when the object is offered for sale that the problem may arise.

There are several reasons for such legislation, the most important being that sterling silver was, until the 1850s, the same standard metal as coin. Another is that silver solder is difficult to detect with the naked eye (it may be visible when breathed upon the frosted surface) and it has therefore been possible for unscrupulous craftsmen to considerably alter items of silverware to greatly enhance their value (*see Fakes and Alterations p173*).

Honest repairs should be easily distinguishable. They are likely to occur in obvious places, and a logical and careful examination of the object in question will disclose such evidence. The existence of such repairs should also be reflected in the price. As a general rule it is not advisable to buy repaired silver unless it is the work of a particularly desirable maker or of an exceptionally rare or sought-after type.

GLOSSARY

Alloy A mixture of metals. In silver, the base metals added to strengthen it.

Annealing The process by which silver is heated and then rapidly cooled in order to soften it sufficiently to be workable.

Applied Decoration made separately and added, rather than integral to form.

Apostle spoon A silver spoon with a finial moulded as the figure of one of the Apostles; particularly popular in the 16th century and 17th century.

Argyll A small pot or jug for serving gravy, attributed to the Duke of Argyll in the 18th century. The usual form has a lining or lower section for hot water; another type has a sleeve which contains a heated iron rod. Designs followed fashionable forms from the 1770s until *c*.1830. Examples with their internal insulators removed are occasionally found passed off as bachelor's teapots.

Armorial Generally meaning concerning heraldry or heraldic arms, this term is often used loosely to describe a crest or coat of arms. (*see p86*).

Assay The testing of metal to establish its purity. (*see pp6-7*)

Assay Master The person elected annually to supervise the assay of silver, also called the master of touch or touch warden (*see pp6-11*).

Baluster The term describing a double curved form that swells at the base and rises in a concave curve to a narrow stem or neck, popular during the 18th century when all types of domestic wares appeared in baluster form.

Baroque A highly ornamental style of architecture and decorative art that flourished in Renaissance Europe from the late 16th century.

Bayonet fitting A method of joining covers to bases, particularly of casters, with small lugs twisting into slots, similar in principle to a light bulb fitting.

Beading A decorative border of tight beads, either cast and applied, or embossed.

Bezel The groove or inner rim of a cover – for example on coffee pots and teapots; often the site of the cover marks.

Biggin The small cylindrical coffee or hot water jug with a short spout and domed cover made in the late 18th century.

Bleeding bowl A shallow dish or bowl, the lip of which has an indent to accommodate the neck or other part of the human body. Otherwise known as a barber's or shaving bowl.

Blind caster A caster with an unpierced, engraved cover, probably used to contain dry mustard.

Brandy saucepan Small saucepan, usually with a handle at right angles to the spout. Used for heating brandy, as its name implies.

Bright-cut A type of decorative effect achieved by engraving a faceted design that stands out sharply (*see p84*).

Britannia Standard The highest quantity of silver used in the making of wrought plate, being 95.84%. The Britannia Standard replaced the sterling standard (92.5%) in 1697 and remained in use until 1720, after which it was an optional extra; it is denoted by marks depicting a lion's head erased and the figure of Britannia. (*See pp9-11*)

Britannia metal An alloy of tin, antimony and a trace of copper. A popular 19th century pewter substitute, from *c.*1840 it was widely used as a base for electroplating.

Burnishing An early method of polishing metals, including silver, by applying friction with a hard tool made of agate to create a lustre.

Campana An exaggerated vase shape with a pronounced waist, similar to an upside-down bell.

Canteen Originally, a box containing knives, forks and spoons, but often used to denote a full service of cutlery.

Cartouche The decorative frame surrounding a coat of arms (*see p86*).

Cast Of silver, shaped by pouring molten metal into a mould or cast made from sand, plaster, metal or cuttlefish (*see p81*).

Caster A container for salt, pepper or sugar, with a pierced cover for sprinkling; those intended for spices were often called muffineers after the popularity of the muffin.

Chafing dish Originally a dish with a charcoal burner that kept plates hot, but now applied to a dish used for cooking at the table.

Chalice The wine cup used at Christian communion services. Originally of Catholic origin, they had to be used secretly in England during periods of Catholic intolerance. These recusant chalices were often designed to be easily dismantled and hidden, and tend to be incompletely marked.

Charger A large circular or oval dish or plate, usually richly decorated.

Chasing The detail on embossed work or cast items, worked with a hammer and punches (*see p82*).

Chinoiserie Decoration consisting of naive figures and scenes in an Oriental style that permeated Europe from the Far East; prevalent in the late-17th century, again in the mid-18th century and continuing through into the 19th century (viz Brighton Pavilion); becoming more naturalistic in later periods.

Clipping The unlawful process, common in England until the mid-17th century, whereby a small sliver of silver was pared from the edge of the unmilled coinage.

Close plating A method of applying a layer of precious metal foil to steel, sometimes used by cutlers to protect steel knives from staining (*see p85*).

Commonwealth The term used to describe the period between 1649 and 1660 when England was ruled by Oliver Cromwell as Lord Protector.

Crockets A type of formalized scrolling leaf-shaped carving, usually applied to outer edges of silver decorated with Gothic arches and spires.

Cruet A frame for holding casters and condiment bottles at the table.

Cut-card decoration Flat shapes of applied silver, mostly in the form of leaves, *fleur-de-lys* or trefoil, used as decoration and reinforcement, especially around the rims or bases of tea and coffee pots (*see p82*).

Date letter The present-day name for the mark first introduced to identify the assay master, depicted by a letter of the alphabet.

Die-stamping The production of patterned silver by the use of "male" and "female" dies pressed together on either side of sheet silver. Introduced *c.*mid-18th century, the process facilitated the mass-production of elaborate silver.

Dish ring A ring used to keep hot plates away from the table surface. Usually with concave sides pierced with animal shapes, dish rings are today given blue glass liners and used as dessert baskets. Also called a pototo ring.

Display silver Huge and elaborate articles made with the express purpose of exhibiting the wealth of the owner.

Drip-pan The detachable part of a candlestick which contains the candle and catches the drips of wax. The drip pan fits into the nozzle or sconce.

Duty dodging The practice of taking marks from one small assayed piece of silver and inserting them into a much larger piece in order to avoid paying duty on the weight of the larger article; prevalent between 1784 and 1890, when a hefty duty was levied on silver (*see p16*).

Duty mark The mark applied to all silverware from 1784 to 1890 (with a few exceptions – *see p10*), representing the sovereign's head, to signify that duty had been paid.

Electroplating The application of a layer of pure silver to a base metal (initially copper and later Britannia metal and nickel) using electrolysis, to produced silver plate (*see p85*).

Electrotyping A sophisticated development of electroplating that facilitates the accurate imitation of solid objects (*see p85*).

Embossing A form of relief decoration worked into the silver from both sides with a hammer and/or punch, leaving a raised pattern (*see p83*).

Engraving The incised decoration on metal created without a hammer.

Epergne A large and elaborate centrepiece for a table consisting of a central bowl surrounded by several smaller, detachable bowls, used from the mid-18th century for displaying and serving fruit and sweetmeats.

Erased The heraldic term meaning literally 'torn off at the shoulders' describes pictorial representations of the head only. Not to be confused with erasure (*see below*).

Erasure The removal of an existing coat of arms, crest or engraving, which is sometimes replaced by a new inscription (*see p86*).

Everted Outward-turned or flaring of, for example, a rim.

Ewer A large, lipped jug, often part of a set with a basin. Prior to the introduction of forks, ewers held the water used by diners to wash their hands during meals.

Filigree Fine openwork silver wire decoration, sometimes in panel form or enhanced with little silver beads.

Finial An ornament on top of a spire or gable; hence, the topmost ornament on a piece of silverware (excepting the cover of a cup, which is then called a knop). Also refers to those ends of spoons cast in shapes, such as apostle figures.

Flagon A jug, usually tall and cylindrical, often with religious associations.

Flat chasing A variation of the chasing process whereby the decoration appears in low relief (*see p83*).

Flatware The term for all flat objects, such as plates and salvers, but more specially applied to tableware without a cutting edge (i.e. spoons and forks).

Gadrooning A repeated border pattern composed of a succession of alternating lobes and flutes, usually curved (*see p88*).

Gilding A method of applying a thin layer of gold to silver (*see p85*).

Goldsmith Literally a worker in gold, but from earliest times the term also covered silversmiths. The craft of the gold and silversmith rapidly became segregated into two main categories: largeworker and smallworker Large-workers made wares of substantial size and included candlestick makers and salver makers. Smallworkers made small wares and included bucklemakers, snuffbox makers, spoonmakers, spectaclemakers and watchcasemakers.

Goldsmiths' Company The craft guilds were established to protect the public and honest tradesmen from fraudsters, and to provide a form of guarantee. By the mid-13th century they had developed into an enormously powerful force. Edward III's Act of 1327 acknowledged the Worshipful Company of Goldsmiths, and bestowed upon them the right to enforce the assay laws (*see p7*).

Hallmarks The marks applied to silver to indicate that it has been passed at assay – i.e. confirmed as having the required minimum silver content. The term derives from Goldsmiths' Hall in London, originally the only place where such marks were struck.

Hollow wares Any hollow vessels, jugs, pots or tankards.

Imported plate Foreign silver imported in England was originally assayed on arrival, despite bearing the marks of its country of origin. In 1844 the law changed to allow foreign silverware made before 1800 to be imported without having hallmarks added. Post-1800 pieces still had to be assayed at the port of entry. No identifying mark for this later plate was introduced until 1876.

"Improved" Altered at a later date with decoration, a practice common during the 19th century.

Largeworker A maker of salvers, trays, candlesticks, plates, dishes, urns, baskets and other wares of a substantial size. (*See also under Goldsmith*.)

Loading (or filling) A system for strengthening and stabilizing pressed sheet silver wares, whereby an iron rod is fixed inside the body using pitch or plaster. Particularly useful in the production of candlesticks made from pressed sheet silver and similar items requiring stability, and less expensive than casting.

Mantling The background plumage or drapery against which a coat of arms is displayed (*see p88*).

Milled edge The system introduced by Charles II whereby the edges of coins were engraved with grooves or a written legend, in order to discourage the widespread and dishonest practice of coin clipping.

Muffineer See caster.

Mug A drinking vessel without a lid.

Nickel Any of various white alloys of copper, zinc and nickel used as a base for coating with silver using the electroplate method.

Nozzle That part of a candlestick into which the candle is fitted. (*See also "sconce" and "drip-pan".*)

Pap boat A small, shallow bowl with a lip, used for feeding children or invalids in the latter half of the 18th century.

Parcel gilt An early means of describing "partially gilded".

Patina The beautiful, deep, blue-silver lustre that silver aquires with the passage of time and as a result of numerous surface scratches. This effect is lost by machine-polishing. (*See also "skin".*)

Pellet A small star used as a component of some maker's marks.

Plate Originally the term for domestic wares made of silver and gold, the term is now commonly confused with Sheffield plate, leading to the mistaken idea that early wrought plate was plated.

Plateworker A general term to describe a silversmith.

Raising The process by which a piece of hollow ware is hammered into shape using annealed silver.

Repoussé Meaning "pushed out", a form of embossing, whereby the embossed metal is then chased in order to refine the design (*see p82*).

Revocation of the Edict of Nantes The Edict of Nantes, promulgated by Henry IV in 1598, granted freedom of religion to French Protestants. Its Revocation by Louis XIV in 1685 led to hoards of French Protestants fleeing religious persecution and settling in Great Britain, among them large numbers of Huguenot craftsmen, including silversmiths.

Rococo An architectural and decorative style that originated in early 18th century France and spread throughout Europe, characterized by elegant, elaborate decoration.

Salt The collectors' term for a salt cellar.

Salver A flat dish, usually with feet, similar to a tray but smaller and without handles.

Sconce Variously, the candle socket of any candle holder, a type of bracket candle holder attached to a wall, and a flat candlestick with a handle.

Scratch weight A note made of the weight, in ounces and pennyweights troy, of an article at assay, usually hand engraved lightly on the base or reverse.

Sheet Sheet silver and sheet metal describe the panels of silver and plate used in the manufacture of silverwares. As distinct from cast silver.

Sheffield plate (or fused plate) The fusion of sheet sterling silver and a base metal alloy, usually copper, used as a silver substitute (*see p168*).

Smallworker A maker of small wares, such as snuff boxes, buckles, vinaigrettes and wine labels. (*See also Goldsmith.*)

Soy frame Similar to a cruet, a frame to hold small bottles of sauce.

Sterling silver The purity standard for British silver, namely 92.5% pure silver. First set in the reign of Henry II (1154–1189) it is still in use today.

Strapwork A decorative method probably brought to England by Huguenot craftsmen and consisting of interlacing straps or bands of ornament. These were originally engraved but, by the end of the 17th century, cast and applied in a more elaborate form. Also describes a type of formal design.

Tankard Large mug with a hinged lid and thumbpiece for drinking beer.

Tazza A type of salver on a raised central stand.

Thumbpiece The flange attached to a hinged lid which, when pressed by the thumb, raises the lid.

Touch Originally, the test by touchstone to discover the purity of metal before recieving the mark of the assay office.

Touchstone A hard, dark, siliceous stone (perhaps basalt or jasper) used to test the quality of gold and silver.

Trefid A 17th-century spoon, the handle of which terminates in a bud shape, usually cleft into a central stem and two lobes.

Trefoil The term describing decorative motifs with three leaves or lobes.

Troy A system to measure the weight of precious stones and metals first used at Troyes in France. The system is based on the weight of a grain. 24 grains = 1 pennyweight. 20 pennyweights = 1 troy ounce. 12 ounces = 1 troy pound.

Worshipful Company of Goldsmiths The ancient company of the City of London established to represent those involved in gold and silversmithing.

Wrought plate The ancient and general term for all silverware and gold made by hand.

BIBLIOGRAPHY

Assay Offices of Great Britain *Hallmarks on Gold Silver & Platinum*

Banister, Judith ed. *English Silver Hall-Marks, Including the Marks of Origin on Scottish and Irish Silver Plate, Gold, Platinum and Sheffield Plate from Circa 1554* W. Foulsham & Co. Ltd 1990

Bly, John *Discovering Hallmarks on English Silver* Shire 1968

Bly, John ed. *Is is Genuine?* Mitchell Beazley 1986

Bradbury, Frederick *Bradbury's Book of Hallmarks: Old Sheffield Plate Maker's Marks 1743 to 1860* J.W. Northend Ltd Publications 1969

Brett, Vanessa *The Sotheby's Directory of Silver 1600-1940,* Sotheby's Publications 1986

Bruton, Eric *Hallmarks and Date Letters on Silver, Gold and Platinum* N A G Press 1944

Culme, John *The Directory of Gold and Silversmiths, Jewellers and Allied Traders 1838-1914* Antique Collectors' Club 1987

Davis, Frank *French Silver 1450-1825,* Arthur Barker Ltd 1970

Divis, Jan *Silver Marks of the World,* Hamlyn 1976

Feild Rachael *Buying Antique Silver and Sheffield Plate* Macdonald Orbis 1988

Green, Robert Alan *Marks of American Silversmiths* Murphy 1977

Grimwade, Arthur G. *London Goldsmiths 1697-1837. Their Marks & Lives,* Faber and Faber 1976

Jackson, Sir Charles J. *English Goldsmiths and their Marks,* Dover 1921

Kovel, Ralph M. & Terry H. *A Directory of American Silver, Pewter and Silver Plate* Crown 1979

Langford, Joel *Silver A Practical Guide to Collecting Silverware and Identifying Hallmarks,* The Apple Press 1991

Pickford, Ian ed. *Jackson's Hallmarks English, Scottish, Irish Silver & Gold Marks from 1300 to the Present Day –* Pocket Edition Antique Collectors' Club 1991

Miller, Judith & Martin ed. *Miller's Pocket Antiques Fact File* Mitchell Beazley 1988

Miller, Judith & Martin ed. *Miller's Understanding Antiques,* Mitchell Beazley 1989

Strong, Roy *The Collector's Encyclopedia: Victoriana to Art Deco* Collins 1974

Tardy *International Hallmarks on Silver* Tardy, Paris 1981

Waldron, Peter *The Price Guide to Antique Silver* Antique Collectors' Club 1988

LIST OF USEFUL ADDRESSES

The Assay Office
Goldsmiths' Hall
Gutter Lane
London E2V 8AQ

The Assay Office
137 Portobello Street
Sheffield S1 4DR

The Assay Office
Newhall Street
Birmingham B3 1SB

The Assay Office
15 Queen Street
Edinburgh EH2 1JE

British Antiques Dealers' Association
(BADA)
20 Rutland Gate
London SW7 1BD
Tel 071 589 4128

London and Provincial Antique Dealers' Association (LAPADA)
Suite 214
535 Kings Road, London SW10 0SZ
Tel 071 823 3511

"Adam" silverware 90
alloys 6
alterations 172, 173-4
American silver 91, 162
annealing 6, 81
Antique Plate Committee 15, 172
apostle spoons 178
applied decoration 81-3
argylls 178
armorials 86-8, 174
assay offices 18-46

baskets, cake 92
beaded borders 91
"berry" spoons 178
borders 87-8
brandy saucepans 178
bright-cut engraving 84
Britannia silver standard 9-11

cake baskets 92
Canadian silver 91
candelabra 93, 175
candlesticks 93-4, 175, 181
caring for silver 180-1
cartouches 87-8
cast decoration 81-3
casters 94-5
centrepieces 98
chasing 82-3
chocolate pots 95-6
church silver 16-17
cleaning 180-1
clipping 9
close plating 85
coats of arms 86-7, 174
coffee pots 95-6, 179
collecting 180-2
colonial silver 14-15
Commonwealth silver 89
Continental European silver 15, 155-62
convention marks 11
copper alloys 6
cow creamers 175-6
cream jugs 176
crests 86-7
cruets 96-7
cups, two-handled 105-6
cut-card decoration 82

date letter system 8, 180
Deacon's marks 12, 13
decoration 81-5
dishes 176-7
duty dodgers 16

ecclesiastical silver 16-17
electroplating 85, 108
electrotyping 85
embossing 83
Empire style 87
engraving 83-4
entrée dishes 97
EPBM (electroplated Britannia metal) 81, 85
epergnes 98
EPNS (electroplated nickel silver) 81, 85
European hallmarking 13-14, 47-80

fakes 172-9
flat chasing 83
forged hallmarks 173
frosting 173
funnels, wine 106, 179

gadroon borders 90, 91
gilding 85
gold hallmarking 166-7
Goldsmiths' Company 7-8

Hallmarking Act (1973) 11-12, 15
hammering 84-5
Huguenots 10, 89

imported silver 15-16
initials 87
inscriptions 87
Irish silver 12-13, 91

jugs 98-9, 176

King's mark 7

ladles 178
leopard's head 7, 8-9
lion's head 9
lion passant 8
loading 81

maker's marks 10
manufacture 81
"milling" 9

neo-classicism 90

planishing 84-5
plates 176-7
platinum hallmarking 167
porringers 175-6
pouncing 85
raising 81

Regency style 90
repairs 181-2
replicas 172
repoussé 82-3
Restoration silver 90
rococo style 90
rolling 81

salts 99-100, 181
salvers 100-1, 177
sauce boats 101-2, 177
Scottish silver 12-13
scratchweight 174
scrolled borders 90, 91
Sheffield plate 168-71
shell borders 90, 91
silver standard 6-9
snuffers 175
solder 181-2
spoons 16, 102, 177-8, 180
strapwork 82
styles, silver 92-106
substitutes 85
sugar basins 178
surface treatments 84-5

table silver 177-8
tankards 103, 178-9
taxes 10-11, 16
tazzas 177
tea kettles 179
teapots 103-4, 179
thread borders 88
transposed hallmarks 16, 173
trays 177
tureens 104-5, 177
two-handled cups 105-6

unmarked wares 15, 172

waiters 100-1
wine funnels 106, 179
wrought silver 6, 81

INDEX OF TOWNS AND MAKERS

A-Z list of Continental makers not included in index below
159-62

A-Z list of American makers not included in index below
164-165

Aalborg 50
Aarhus 51, 77
Abdy, William 114
Abercromby, Robert 114
Adams, George W. 114
Adams, Stephen 114
Aix 55
Aldridge, Charles 114
Aldridge, Edward 114
Alexander, William 114
Allen, Joseph 114
Amien 56
Amsterdam 67, 68
Angell, George & John Charles 115
Angell, John 114-15
Angell, Joseph 115
Angers 56
Annesley, Arthur 115
Antwerp 47
Archambo, Peter jnr 115
Archambo, Peter snr 115
Arnett, Hugh 115
Arnhem 67, 68
Ashbee, Charles Robert 107
Asprey & Co. Ltd 107
Astrakhan 73
Atkinson, William 115
Augsburg 62
Auguste, Henry 155
Auguste, Robert Joseph 155
Austria 14

Bagnall, William 115
Bair, Melchior 155
Balzac, Edmé-Pierre 155
Bamford, Thomas 115
Barbe, John 115
Barcelona 75
Barnard, Edward 116, 126
Barnard, Edward jnr 116

Barnard, John 116
Barnard, William 116
Barnett, Edward 116
Barnstaple 44
Baskerville, George 116
Bass, James Le 116
Bateman, Ann 116
Bateman, Hester 84, 107-8
Bateman, Jonathan 116
Bateman, Peter 116
Bateman, William 116-17
Bates, Samuel 117
Bayley, Richard 117
Beale, George 117
Beale, Richard 117
Belgium 47-50
Bell, Joseph 117
Bell, William 117
Bennett, Edward 117
Bergen 70
Berlin 62
Berthellot, John 117
Besnier, Nicholas 155
Bettridge, John 117
Biennais, Martin Guillaume 155
Bignell, Jonathan 117
Biller, Albrecht 155
Biller, Johann Jakob II 155
Birmingham 21-3
Blackborrow, Samuel 117
Bland, Cornelius 117
Bland, James & Elizabeth 118
Bolton, Thomas 118
Bond, William 118
Boogaert, Thomas 155-6
Boothby, George 118
Bordeaux 56
den Bosch 67, 68
Boulton, Matthew 118, 170
Bouman, Daniel 156
Bradbury, Thomas & Sons 118
Bradshaw, Bennett & Co. 118
Braga 71
Brandt, Reynier 156
Bridge, John 118
Brind, Walter 118
Bristol 44
Brokesby, Abel 118
Brooker, James 119
Brown, Robert 119

Bruges 47
Brussels 48
Bumfriss, Thomas 119
Bunn, Lockington 149
Burridge, Thomas 119
Burrows, Alice & George 119
Burrows, George 141
Burton, Robert 119
Burwash, William 119
Busch, Esaias III 156
Buteux, Abraham 119
Buteux, Elizabeth 119
Butty, Francis 119, 133

Cachart, Elias 119
Cafe, John 108
Cafe, William 119
Calame, James Anthony 120
Caldecott, William 120
Callard, Isaac 120
Callard, Paul 120
Canada 79-80
Capper, Edward 120
Carlisle 44
Carr, Alwyn 111
Carrington & Co. 120
Carter, John 120
Carter, Richard 120, 138
Cartwright, Benjamin 120
Castle, Peter 131
Causton, Thomas 120
Chawner, Henry 120
Chawner, Mary 120
Chawner, Thomas 121
Chawner, William 121, 132
Chester 23-6
Chesterman, Charles 121
Clark, Thomas 121
Coates, Alexander 121
Coimbra 71
Coker, Ebenezer 121
Cologne 62
Comyns, William & Sons 121
Cooke, Edward 121

Cooper, Matthew 121
Cope, C.G. 170
Copenhagen 50
Cordoba 75
Cotton, John 121
Courtauld, Augustine 121
Courtauld, Louisa Perina 122
Courtauld, Samuel 122
Courtauld family 108
Coventry 44
Cowles, George 122
Cowper, Henry 122
Cox, Robert Albin 122
Cradock, Joseph 122, 130
Craig, Ann 122
Crespell, Sebastian & James 122-3
Crespin, Paul 123
Creswick, Fenton & Co. 123
Creswick, T. & J. 170
Cripps, Mark 123
Cripps, William 123
Crossley, Richard 123, 148
Crouch, John 131
Crouch, John jnr 123
Cruickshank, Robert 123
Crump, Francis 123, 147

Dalton, Isaac 123
Daniell, Jabez 124
Daniell, Thomas 124
Dantzig 62
Darker, William 124
Davenport, Burrage 124
Davenport, Isaac 124
Davenport, Samuel 124
De Oliveyra, Abraham 124
Delft 68
Delisle, Louis 124
Delmestre, John 124
Denmark 50-1
Devonshire, Thomas 124
Dijon 57
Dixon, James & Sons 124, 170
Dixon, T. & Co.170
Dobson, J.W. 124-5
D'Olier, Isaac 139
Dorrell, Jane 125
Dortrecht 68
Dresden 62
Dresser, Christopher 108

Dublin 26-9
Duguay, Joseph-Pierre-Jacques 156
Dulliker, Johann Jakob 156
Dumée, Nicholas 119, 134
Dummer, Jeremiah 163
Dupont, Louis 125
Düsseldorf 62

East, John 125
Eaton, Elizabeth 125
Eaton, William 125
Edinburgh 29-32
Edington, James Charles 125
Edwards, Edward 125
Edwards, John 125, 126
Edwards, William 125-6
Eelioet, Franssoys 156
Egan, Daniel 126
Eley, William jnr 126
Eley, William snr 126
Elkington, George 85
Elkington & Co. 108-9
Ellerby, W. 170
Elliott, William 126, 148
Emes, John 126
Emes, Rebecca 126
England, Thomas 126-7
Essen 62
Eustace, Thomas 127
Evora 71
Exeter 32-4

Fairburn, G. 171
Faro 71
Fawdery, William 127
Fearn, William 126
Feline, Edward 127
Fenton Brothers Ltd 127
Fernell, Edward 127, 130
Fletcher, Bernard 127
Florence 66
Fogelberg, Andrew 109, 127
Fossey, John 127
Foster, Thomas 127
Fountain, John 127
Fountain, William 128
Fox, Charles jnr 128
Fox, Charles Thomas 128

Fox, George 128
Fox, Mordecai 114
France 13-14, 51-61
Frankfurt 63
Fray, John 153
Freeman, Thomas 128
Freeth, H. 170
French, Edward 121
Frisbee, William 128
Frost, John 128
Fuller, Crispin 128

Gafle 77
Gamble, William 128
Garden, Phillip 128-9
Gardy, Joseph 131
Garnett, W. 170
Garrard, Robert 109
Garrard, William 129
Geneva 78
Genoa 66
Germain, François-Thomas 156
Germain, Pierre 156
Germain, Thomas 156
Germany 14, 61-5
Gérona 75
Ghent 48
Gilbert, J. 170
Gilbert, Stephen 127
Giles, George 129
Gillingham, George 129
Gilpin, Thomas 129
Gladwin, Thomas 129
Glasgow 34-6
Godbehere, Samuel 129
Goddard, Philip 129
Godfrey, Benjamin 129
Godfrey, Eliza 109
Godwin, Benjamin 129
Gorham Manufacturing Co. 163
Gosling, Richard 130
Gouda 68
Gould, James 130
Gould, William 130
Green, Henry 114
Green, Samuel 130
Greene, Henry 130
Grenoble 57
Grundy, William 130
Guest, James 130
Guest, Thomas 130
Guichard, Louis 130
Guimaraes 71
Gulliver, Nathaniel 130

Gurney, Richard & Co. 131
Gwillim, William 131

The Hague 68
Hall, Martin & Co. 131
Hall, William 131, 170
Hallsworth, Henry 131
Hamburg 63
Hamilton, John 131
Hamon, Lewis 131
Hancock, Joseph 170
Hancock, Messrs & Co. 131
Hannam, Thomas 131
Hanover 63
Harrison Bros & Howson 132
Harvey, John 132
Harwood, Samuel 132
Harwood, T. 170
Hatfield, Charles 132
Hawksworth, Eyre & Co. 132
Hayter, Thomas 147
Hayter, Thomas & George 132
Head, Thomas 121
Heming, George 132
Heming, Thomas 132
Hennell, David 132-3
Hennell, Robert 133
Hennell, Samuel 133
Hennell family 110
Herbert, Henry 133
Herbert, Samuel 133
Herne, Lewis 133
Hill, Ann 133
Hindmarsh, George 114, 134
Hitchcock, Samuel 134
Hodgkins, William 138
Holaday, Sarah 134
Holland, H. & Co. 170
Holmes, William 134
Hopkins, John 134
Hougham, Charles 134
Howard, S. & T. 170
Howland, Solomon 134
Hull 44-5
Humphreys, Arthur 142
Hunt, John S. 134

Hutton, Samuel 134
Hutton, W. 171
Hyatt, John 134

Ireland 88
Italy 65-7

Jackson, Orlando 119
Jacobs, John 134
Jay, Edward 135
Jury, William 114

Kalmar 76
Kandler, Charles Frederick 135
Karlstad 77
Keating, James 135
Kiev 73
King, David 135
King, Jeremiah 135
King, William 135
King's Lynn 45
Knox, Archibald 110
Königsberg 63

Lake, Henry 135
Lambe, Edward 135
Lambe, George 135
Lambe, Jane 135
Lambe, John 135
Lamerie, Paul de 90, 110
Lampfert, John 136
Langford, John 136
Langlois, James 136
Laroche, Louis 136
Laughlin, John 136
Laundy, Samuel 136
Lausanne 79
Law, R. 171
Le Francis, Abraham 136
Le Sage, Augustin 136
Le Sage, John Hugh 136
Le Sage, Simon 136-7
Lea, A.C. 171
Leader, Thomas & Daniel 136
Leeds 45
Lehendrick, Louis-Joseph 156-7
Leicester 45
Leipzig 63
Leslie, Charles 137
Lewes 45
Lias, Charles 137
Lias, John & Henry 137
Liège 48
Lille 57
Lincoln 45
Lingard, John 137
Lisbon 72
Lofthouse, Mary 137
Lofthouse, Matthew 137
Lofthouse, Seth 137

Loir, Alexis III 157
London 18-21
Looker, William 137
Louvain 48
Love, J. & Co. 171
Lowe, Edward 137
Lowndes, Thomas 131
Lubeck 63
Lucas, Robert 137
Ludlow, John 137
Luneburg 64
Luzern 79
Lyons 57

Maastricht 68
Madden, Jonathan 137
Madrid 75
Magdeburg 64
Maitland, James 138
Makepeace, Robert 138
Malmo 76, 77
Mann, Thomas 138
Manners, James 138
Mannheim 64
Mappin & Webb 138
Marshall, John 128
May, Richard 125
Mercer, Thomas 138
Meredith, H. 171
Methuen, George 138
Metz 57-8
Meure, Peter 115
Milan 66
Mills, Nathaniel 138
Mince, James 138
Mons 48
Montpellier 58
Moore, J. 171
Moore, Thomas 138
Morison, James 139
Moscow 73
Motherby, John 139
Munich 64

Nancy 58
Nantes 58
Naples 66
Neill, J.R. 139
Nelme, Anthony 139
Nelme, Francis 139
Netherlands 67-9
Neuville 79
Neville, John 122
Newcastle 36-8
Niewenhuys, Hendrik 157
Nora 77
Northcote, Hannah 139
Northcote, Thomas 139
Norway 69-71
Norwich 39
Novgorod 74

Nuremburg 64
Nutting, Henry 139

Odense 51
Odessa 74
Odiot, Jean-
Baptiste-Claude
157
Oporto 72
Orebro 76
Orleans 58
Oslo 70
Outrebon, Jean-
Louis-Dieudonne
157

Pages, Francis 139
Palermo 66
Pantin, Simon 139-
40
Pargeter, Richard
140
Paris 53-5
Parker, John 140
Parr, Thomas 140
Parsons, A. & F. 140
Payne, Humphrey
140
Payne, John 140
Payne, Thomas &
Richard 140
Pearce, Edmund 140
Pearce, Richard 141
Peaston, William &
Robert 141
Peterson, Abraham
141
Petrograd 74
Phillips, S.J. 141
Phillis, Phillip 141
Phipps, John 118
Phipps, Thomas 141
Pilleau, Pezé 141
Pitches, George 126
Pittar, John 141
Pitts, William 141
Platel, Pierre 89,
111
Playfair, William 141
Plumley, Charles &
John 142
Plummer, William
142
Plymouth 46
Pocock, Edward
115
Podio, Peter 142
Poitiers 59
Pont, Jan Diederik
157
Poole 46
Portugal 71-2
Pratt, Thomas
Boulton 142
Preedy, Joseph 141,
142
Priest, John 142
Priest, William 146
Priest, William &
James 142
Prussia 65

Purdee, Edwin
Charles 142
Pyne, Benjamin 142

Quantock, John 142

Rainaud, Philip 143
Ram, Abel 143
Ramsden, Omar 111
Rawlings, Charles
143
Regensburg 65
Reid, William 122
Reily, Charles 143
Reims 59
Rennes 59
Revere, Paul jnr 163
Ribouleau, Isaac 143
Richardson, Richard
143
Ridout, George 143
Riom 59
Ritter family 157
Roberts, Cadman
& Co. 171
Roberts, J. & S.171
Roberts & Belk 143
Robins, Thomas 143
Robinson, Edward
141
Robinson, John 143
La Rochelle 59-60
Roettiers, Jacques
157
Roettiers, Jacques-
Nicholas 157-8
Roker, Elizabeth
144
Roker, John 144
Roker, Matthew 144
Roker, Philip 144
Romania 14
Rome 66
Romer, Emick 144
Rongent, Etienne
144
Rood, Mary 144
Roode, Gundry 144
Roose, Alexander
144
Rotterdam 68
Rouen 60
Rugg, Richard 144
Rundell, Philip 144-5
Rundell Bridge &
Rundell 111
Russia 14, 72-5

Sadler, Thomas 145
Sala 77
Salisbury 46
Sampel, William 116
Sanders, Joseph 145
Sanderson, Robert
164
Savory Adey, Joseph
& Albert 145
Scarlett, Richard
145
Scarlett, William
145

Schiotling, Johannes
158
Schofield, John 145
Schofield, William
145
Schuppe, John 145,
175
Scofield, John 146
Scott, Digby 146
Sebille, John 136
Semore, Charles
134
Sharp, Robert 120,
147
Shaw, William 146
Sheene, Alice 146
Sheffield 39-41
Sherborne 46
Shermer, Thomas
146
Shruder, James 146
Sibley, Richard 119,
146
Silkirk, W. 171
Simons, William 146
Slater, James 146
Sleamaker, Daniel
146-7
Sleath, Gabriel 147
Smiley, William
Robert 147
Smit, Jan 158
Smith, Benjamin
111-12, 146
Smith, Daniel 120,
147
Smith, George 123,
147
Smith, James 147
Smith, Nathaniel &
Co. 147
Smith, Robarts &
Co. 171
Smith, S.W. & Co.
147-8
Soame, William 148
Spain 75
Spilsbury, Francis
148
Spilsbury, Francis jnr
148
Sprimont, Nicholas
148
Squire, George 148
Stamper, John 114
Stevenson, Ambrose
148
Stockholm 76
Stone, John 148
Storer, George 143
Storr, Paul 112
Story, J.W. 148
Strant, Willem 158
Strasbourg 60, 65
Stuttgart 65
Summers, William
143
Sumner, William
148
Sutton, William 148
Sweden 14, 75-8

Swift, John 149
Switzerland 14, 78-9

Tanqueray, Ann 149
Tanqueray, David 149
Tant, William 149
Taunton 46
Tayler, John 149
Taylor, Joseph Hayes 149
Taylor, Samuel 149
Tearle, Thomas 149
Terroux, Etienne 158
Tessier, Edward 140
Thellott, Johann Andreas 158
Theobalds, William 149
Thomas & Co. 149
Tiffany Co. 164
Toledo 75
Tookey, Elizabeth 150
Tookey, James 150
Tookey, Thomas 150
Toulouse 60
Tournai 49
Tours 60-1
Townsend, Charles 150
Trondheim 70
Truro 46
Tudor & Leader 150, 171
Tuite, John 150
Tuite, William 150
Turin 67
Tweedie, Walter 150

Uberlingen 65
Ulm 65
Unite, George 150
USA 14-15, 79, 162-5
Utrecht 68

Van Vianen, Christian 158
Venice 67
Vevey 79
Viborg 51
Videau, Aymé 150
Vincent, Edward 151
Vladimir 74
Vries, Jan de 158

Wakelin, Edward 140, 151
Wakelin, John 151
Wakley, Thomas 152
Walker, Joseph 151
Walker, Matthew 151
Walker, Thomas 151
Walker & Hall 151-2
Wall, John 124
Wallis, Thomas 152
Walsh, Matthew 152
Walsh, Michael 152
Ward, Joseph 152
Waterhouse, Hatfield & Co. 171
Watkins, William 124
Watson, J. & Son 171
Watts, Benjamin 152
Watts, Richard 152
Weir & Rogers 152
Welder, Samuel 152
West, Alderman & Co. 152
West, Benjamin 152
West, M. & Sons 152
West, William 152
Wheeler, Frank Clarke 151
Wheeler, Gervase 152
Whipham, Thomas 153

White, Fuller 153
Whitford, Samuel & George 153
Wickes, George 112
Wiener Werkstätte 158
Wilkes Barker, Christopher & Thomas 153
Wilkinson, D. Holy & Co. 171
Wilks, Denis 153
Wilks, James 153
Willaume, David jnr 153
Willaume, David snr 153
Williamson, William 153
Willmott, James 153
Wilson, William 141
Wimbush, Thomas 153
Wintle, Samuel 154
Wood, Edward 154
Wood, Samuel 154
Woods, Christopher 154
Woodward, John 154
Woodward, W. 171
Woodward, William 154
Wright, Charles 154
Wright, J. 171

Yapp, John 154
York 41-3
Young, James 154
Younge, John & Co. 154
Younge, S. & C. & Co. 171
Ypres 49
Ystad 77

Zouch, Richard 154
Zurich 79
Zwolle 68

ACKNOWLEDGEMENTS

Thanks are due to the following for their help in the preparation of this book:

Harry Charteris, Sotheby's London

The Goldsmiths' Hall, London

Asprey & Co. Ltd, London